AT HOME WITH YOUR PC

Joe Kraynak

alpha books

A Division of Prentice Hall Computer Publishing
11711 North College, Carmel, Indiana 46032 USA

To my brothers Greg and John, and to my wife, Cecie, who, without realizing it, gave me the idea for this book.

International Standard Book Number: 0-672-30187-3
Library of Congress Catalog Card Number: 92-61030

95 94 93 92   8 7 6 5 4 3 2 1

Interpretation of the printing code: the rightmost double-digit number is the year of the book's printing; the rightmost single-digit number is the number of the book's printing. For example, a printing code of 92-1 shows that the first printing of the book was in 1992.

Screen reproductions in this book were created by means of the program Collage Plus from Inner Media, Inc., Hollis, NH.

Printed in the United States of America

Marie Butler-Knight
PUBLISHER

Elizabeth Keaffaber
MANAGING EDITOR

Lisa A. Bucki
PRODUCT DEVELOPMENT MANAGER

Faithe Wempen
DEVELOPMENT EDITOR

Linda Hawkins
SENIOR PRODUCTION EDITOR

Albright Communications, Incorporated
MANUSCRIPT EDITOR

San Dee Phillips, Hilary J. Adams, and Martha Norris
EDITORIAL ASSISTANTS

Bill Henderickson
COVER AND INTERIOR DESIGN

Joelynn Gifford
INDEXER

Carla Hall-Batton, Brad Chinn, Terri Edwards, Mark Enochs,
Kate Godfrey, John Kane, Juli Pavey, Linda Quigley,
Joe Ramon, Angie Trzepacz, and Julie Walker
PRODUCTION TEAM

SPECIAL THANKS

To C. Herbert Feltner
for ensuring the
technical accuracy
of this book.

CONTENTS

INTRODUCTiON

If you're anything like me, you bought a computer because you thought you *should* have one. If you didn't have a computer in your house, your kids might turn out to be idiots. Or maybe some punk right out of college would nab your job just because he knew how to use a computer.

Whatever the reason, now you have it. And it sits there next to that set of encyclopedias you bought when your first child was due. You keep staring at it and thinking of the wonderful things you could have bought with that one or two thousand dollars: a new roof for your house, maybe a new CD player and a hundred CDs, maybe even a good used car. Like the cave dweller who invented the wheel, you know that you have a powerful machine in your house, but you haven't yet realized what it's good for.

This book shows you what your computer is good for: how you can use the computer in your home to do your taxes; create resumes; keep an address book; look up recipes; keep track of your schedule; create banners, signs, and greeting cards; get news and weather reports, and more! You learn what's out there in the computer world and how it can improve your life.

WHAT THIS BOOK IS AND WHAT IT IS NOT Whenever you buy a computer, a program, a book, or even a car, you should know what you're getting . . . and what you're not getting. First, here's a list of what you're *not* getting:

- A *Buyer's Guide*. This book does not compare various programs in each category and tell you which one's best. That would take several hundred more pages and is best left to magazine articles.

- A *How-To Book*. This book doesn't show you step-by-step how to use a program. Instead, this book shows you some of the neat features each program offers.

- A *General Computing Book*. This book does not go into the various categories of software—word processing, spreadsheet, database, desktop publishing, graphics, and so on. For that, see my *First Book of Personal Computing*.

What this book *is* is a tour guide through programs and devices that have a special place in the home. To write this book, I made a list of things people commonly do in the home, such as cooking, keeping a calendar, addressing envelopes, writing letters, shopping, figuring taxes, and planning a vacation. I then looked at programs designed specifically to help automate these tasks. And I found scores of programs. I even found programs for household tasks I hadn't thought of: deciding which movie to rent, getting information about your health, and learning how to type.

I chose one program from each category to represent that category. This book shows how each program works and what it can do for you. I think you will be amazed at some of the programs on the market, and you will begin to see how you can make your computer earn its keep.

ACKNOWLEDGMENTS I'd like to give special thanks to Marie Butler-Knight, founder of Alpha Books, for creating a line of books specifically designed for home users, for asking me to write this book, and for having such a creative mind.

Thanks to the editorial staff at Alpha Books for fine-tuning my manuscript. Thanks to Faithe Wempen, development editor, for her insights, enthusiasm, and direction. Her spoken and unspoken comments helped me develop a sense of audience for this book. Thanks to Herb Feltner for checking the book for technical accuracy and for lending an unintimidating hand whenever I ran into problems. Thanks to Lisa Bucki, Liz Keaffaber, and Linda Hawkins for coordinating the production of the book, and to Nancy Albright, manuscript editor, for tightening my language and fine-tuning my voice.

Thanks also to our wonderful, unheralded production department at Prentice Hall Computer Publishing for transforming a stack of pages into an attractive, bound book.

MAKE YOUR COMPUTER PART OF THE FAMILY

Getting a computer is a lot like getting a dog. You get the computer home, and then you realize you haven't planned for it. The computer doesn't match your living room furniture. Your basement is far too cold, damp, and dusty. And the bedroom is packed. And even if you had a place for it, you're missing the essential furniture—a desk, a chair, and a good lamp. In this chapter, we look at how to find the best place for your computer, how to furnish your work area for comfort, and how to connect all the parts.

LOCATION, LOCATION, LOCATION Real estate agents often say the three most important elements to consider in determining a property's value are: location, location, and location. This is true for computers as well. The perfect location is:

- *Convenient and out of the way.* Put your computer where everyone can get at it, but where no one will trip over it. A family room or den is a good choice.

- *Quiet.* You don't want to be distracted when you are engrossed in a project.

- *Clean, cool, and dry.* Dirt, heat, and moisture damage the computer's electrical components. Don't put the computer in direct sunlight, in a damp basement, or next to the clothes dryer, where lint can pour into its openings.

- *Roomy.* Plan ahead. As you get more stuff for your computer, you will need more room to keep all the stuff organized. Give yourself enough room for a good-sized desk and a bookcase.

- *Near a stable source of power.* Fluctuations in power can damage your computer or your files. Don't plug the computer into an outlet that's on the same circuit as an appliance that hogs current, such as a toaster or a clothes dryer.

- *Near a phone line.* If you buy a modem for your computer, you have to plug the modem into an existing phone jack or install another jack. By housing the computer next to an existing phone line, you save yourself some work later.

GET COMFY Comfort is not a luxury—it is a necessity for your long-term health. And I don't want to sound like your mother, but posture has a lot to do with it. Figure 1.1

TIP

A room of its own. If you plan on claiming a deduction for using part of your home for business, you should put the computer in a room of its own, preferably a room with a door.

shows the proper posture you should assume while working at the computer:

- *Feet on the floor or on a footrest.* Crossing your legs blocks your blood circulation, so keep your feet flat on the floor. If your legs dangle, lower your chair, or use a book or some other flat object as a footrest.

- *Back straight, lower back supported.* Slouching hurts your back muscles. Sit up straight, and make sure your chair supports your lower back. If it doesn't, tuck a small pillow between your lower back and the back of the chair.

- *Top of monitor at or slightly below eye level.* If your monitor is too high, you strain your eye muscles trying to look up at it. If the monitor is too low, you strain your neck and shoulder muscles, and probably will get a nasty headache.

- *Elbows at your side, forearms level with keyboard.* You shouldn't reach for your keyboard. If you do, you'll strain your shoulder muscles. Your forearms should be level with the keyboard or slightly above the keyboard.

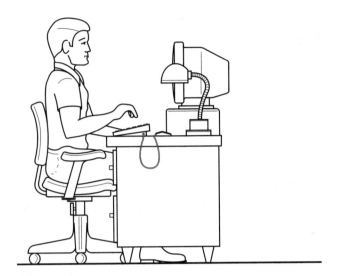

Figure 1.1 Prevent fatigue.

Getting the Right Desk Most desks and tables are too high
for computer keyboards. They're fine for writing or reading, but if your forearms have to reach up to the keyboard,
the desk is too high. The best solution is to purchase a
computer table with an adjustable keyboard platform. (If
you have kids, make sure you can lower the platform or
raise the chair to accommodate them.) If you don't want
to go out and buy a new desk, get an adjustable chair and
raise it.

Getting the Right Chair Speaking of chairs, a chair is the
most important part of your home office furniture. Don't
just get a chair from the kitchen or a cushy chair that

looks comfortable. You want something that supports your body for the arduous task of typing. Here are some guidelines:

- *Adjustability.* All people are built a little differently. Make sure you can adjust the height of the chair, the height of the back support, and the angle of the seat.

- *Back support.* Get a chair that gives you plenty of lower back support. In general, the support should be 6 to 9 inches high and 12 inches wide.

- *Armrests.* I had a chair with armrests. The rests prevented my arms from moving, so I took a hacksaw and chopped them off—the rests, not my arms. If you must have armrests, make sure you can remove them or adjust them.

Shed Some Light on the Subject Getting the proper lighting is tough. You want plenty of light, but not shining directly in your eyes or on your monitor, which will result in glare. Figure 1.2 illustrates how you should try to light your work area.

To determine if you have a problem with glare, turn off your monitor and sit in front of it as you normally would. If you see a light in the monitor, it probably will bother you while you work. Here are some suggestions for reducing glare:

Figure 1.2 Proper lighting reduces eye strain.

- *Change your shirt.* If you wear a white shirt and
  can see it in the monitor, try changing to a
  darker shirt, which reflects less light.

- *Face the monitor at a 90-degree angle to any window.* Windows let in sun, the most intense form

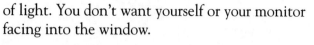

of light. You don't want yourself or your monitor facing into the window.

- *Block the light source that's causing the glare.* You can reduce the lighting at the source (cover the window, turn off the light, or add a light shade). Or you can create a hood for the monitor by taping two manilla folders together, as shown in Figure 1.3.

- *Don't shine a light in the monitor.* If you can see the light bulb in the monitor, you have a problem. Shine the light on a wall that the monitor is facing, or shine it at the ceiling. This gives you indirect lighting.

- *Get an antiglare screen or antiglare UVA glasses.* An antiglare screen fits over your monitor and prevents light from bouncing off the screen into your eyes. Just seeing one in action will sell you on the idea. Usually, the manual that came with your monitor lists its type and size, so that you can find an antiglare screen to match.

- *Adjust the screen brightness.* Most monitors come with *brightness and contrast controls.* Try setting each control to the midrange and then increasing or decreasing the brightness and/or contrast. As a rule of thumb, you want the display to be no brighter than your monitor's plastic border.

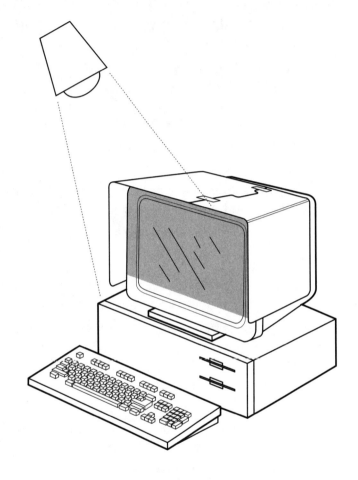

Figure 1.3 A hood eliminates glare.

GETTING YOUR COMPUTER UP AND RUNNING When you get
your computer home and take it out of the box, you
should do three things:

- *Send in all registration and warranty cards* to ensure that you can get technical support for your computer and any software that came with it. This also ensures that if anything goes wrong with your computer, you can get your money back. (Save your receipts, too.)

- *Get a surge protector,* if you don't already have one. A surge protector prevents power fluctuations from damaging the electrical components in the computer.

- *Read the book(s)* that came with your computer to determine how to plug everything in.

If you purchased a used computer and have no books, you can figure out how to connect everything by looking at the back of the computer. Companies usually label the receptacles at the back to show you where to plug in each *peripheral* (keyboard, printer, monitor, and mouse).

The printer and monitor will each have two cords: a cord that connects the unit to the computer and a power cord that plugs into an electrical outlet. Connect the cable to the computer first, before you plug in the electrical cord.

If the receptacles at the back of the computer are not labeled, match the plugs to the receptacles. You need to look for two things. First, make sure one connector has pins and the other connector has holes for pins. If you try to plug pins into pins, you might damage the pins. Second, make sure the number of pins on the plug is the same as the number of holes in the receptacle. It's like plugging a toaster into a wall outlet; you just have to make sure the prongs on the plug fit into the holes in the outlet.

Once you find the proper plug/receptacle pair, gently push the plug into the receptacle. If you have to force it, it's probably not the right fit. If the plug has screws to secure the plug to the receptacle, tighten them (this prevents the plug from falling out). Once all the units are plugged into the computer, plug each unit's electrical cord into your surge protector, and then plug the surge protector into the wall outlet.

Now that you have your computer housed and fed, you are ready to explore the fascinating world of computers.

TIP

Protect your power switches. Turn everything on using the switch on the surge protector. This prevents excess wear and tear on the power switches for the computer, monitor, and printer.

2
WHAT YOU NEED TO KNOW ABOUT DOS

A computer can do a number of different things, but is pretty dumb unless it has some instructions to tell it what to do. The computer needs two types of instructions: operating system software and application software. The operating system tells the computer how to think and communicate. Application software runs on top of the operating system and lets you do such things as type a letter and balance your checkbook. In this chapter, we look at the most commonly used operating system in the home: DOS (pronounced DAWSS).

GETTING STARTED WITH DOS Before you can run any program, you have to *boot* your computer. Boot is a fancy term that means you have to turn on your computer with the disk operating system files in place: the files have to be on your computer's hard disk (if it has one) or on a floppy disk that is in the computer's floppy disk drive A. This procedure is often referred to as the *startup*.

Booting with DOS

1. If your computer does not have a hard disk, insert the DOS startup disk into floppy drive A and close the drive door (if it has a door).

2. Turn on your computer and monitor.

3. If you are asked to enter the date and time, type the date and time as requested or press Enter to accept the date and time that's displayed.

4. Follow any other on-screen messages until you see a *prompt* on-screen that looks something like C:\> or C>.

5. If you booted from a floppy disk, wait until the indicator light next to the disk drive is off and remove the disk.

WORKING WITH DISKS You will store all your program files and the data files you create on disks. If you have a *hard disk*, the disk is usually labeled C. (Most computers have only one hard disk, but it may be treated as several disks: C, D, E, F, and so on.) The *floppy disk drives*, the drives located on the front of your computer, are drives A and B. If your computer has only one floppy drive, it is A and you have no drive B.

TIP
Not sure if the operating system files are in place? Turn on your computer and monitor. If the files are not where your computer can find them, it will display a message on-screen telling you what to do.

Changing to a Disk Drive

1. Make sure there's a *formatted disk* in the drive you want to activate. (Formatting is explained in the next section.)

2. Type the letter of the drive followed by a colon. For example, type `a:`.

3. Press Enter. The DOS prompt changes to show the letter of the drive that is now active.

Before you can store files on a floppy disk, you must format the disk. The formatting procedure creates a map on the disk that later tells DOS where to find the information you stored on it. The following steps explain how to format floppy disks:

Preparing Floppy Disks to Hold Data

1. Change to the drive and directory that contains your DOS files. For example, if your DOS files are in C:\DOS, type `cd\dos` at the C> prompt and press Enter.

2. Insert the blank floppy disk you want to format into floppy drive A or B.

3. Type `format a:` or `format b:` and press Enter.

4. Follow the messages that appear on-screen until you are done.

Whenever you buy a program, the first thing you should do is make *backup copies* of the original program disks. By using backups to install the program, you avoid the risk of damaging the original disks. The following steps explain how to copy program disks:

Copying Disks

1. Obtain a set of blank disks that match the original program disks in number, size, and density. For example, if the program came on three high-density 5.25" disks, obtain three blank high-density 5.25" disks.

2. Change to the drive and directory that contain the DOS program files.

3. Type `diskcopy a: a:` or `diskcopy b: b:`, depending on which drive you're using to make the copies, and press Enter.

4. Follow the on-screen messages until the disk copy operation is complete. (The original disk is the *source disk* and the blank disk is the *target disk*.)

WORKING WITH DIRECTORIES Hard disks hold much more information than floppy disks. To manage the information on a hard disk, store groups of related files in separate directories. Each *directory* acts as a drawer in a filing cabinet (see Figure 2.1).

Before you can work with the files in a given directory, you need to change to that directory. The following steps tell you how:

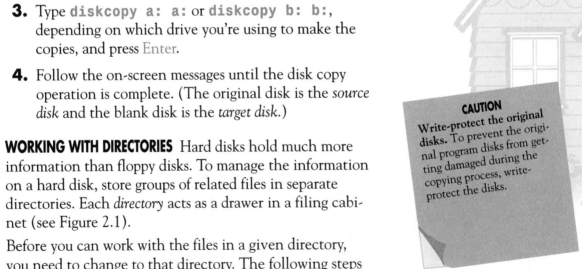

CAUTION
Write-protect the original disks. To prevent the original program disks from getting damaged during the copying process, write-protect the disks.

Each directory can contain
subdirectories and/or files

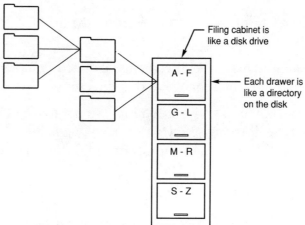

Filing cabinet is
like a disk drive

Each drawer is
like a directory
on the disk

Figure 2.1 Directories store groups of files.

Changing to a Directory

1. Change to the drive that contains the directory. For example, to change to drive C, type `c:` and press Enter.

2. Type `cd\directory`, where *directory* stands for the name of the directory you want to access. (For example, type `cd\dos`.) Press Enter.

The following steps explain how to make directories and how to remove them when they are no longer needed.

Making a Directory

1. Change to the drive you want to create the directory on.

2. If you want to make the directory a subdirectory of another directory, change to that directory.

3. Type `md\`*`directory`*, where *directory* stands for the name of the directory you want to create, up to eight characters. You cannot use any of the following characters:

   " . \ ? [ ] : * < > | + ; , ? space

4. Press Enter. The directory now exists, but you won't see it. To see the new directory, you have to change to it as explained in the earlier section.

Just as you can create directories, you can delete them. However, before you can delete a directory, it must be empty. DOS will not allow you to delete a directory that contains subdirectories and/or files.

Removing a Directory

1. Change to the drive where the directory is located. For example, type `c:` and press Enter.

2. If the directory you want to delete is a subdirectory of another directory, change to the directory above the directory you want to delete. For example, if you want to delete the directory c:\data\letters, type `cd\`**`data`** and press Enter.

16

TIP
No directory name at the prompt? If the DOS prompt does not change to show the current directory, type **prompt pg** and press Enter.

3. Type **rd*directory***, where *directory* stands for the name of the directory you want to delete. For example, type **rd\\letters**. Press Enter.

WORKING WITH FILES Disks contain two types of files: *program files* and *data files*. Program files are the files that contain the instructions that tell the computer how to perform a particular task. Data files are the files you create. For example, if you type a letter and then save it on disk, you create a data file. The following steps explain several procedures for working with files.

Viewing a List of Files

1. Change to the drive and directory that contain the files whose names you want to view.

2. Type **dir** (directory) or **dir/p** (directory/pause) or **dir/w** (directory/wide) and press Enter.

Copying Files

1. Change to the drive and directory that contain the file or files you want to copy.

2. Type the command line:

```
copy filename.ext d:\directory\
```

where *copy* is the DOS COPY command, *filename.ext* is the name of the file you want to copy, and *d:\directory* is the drive letter and directory name you want to copy the file to. (See the examples in Table 2.1.)

3. Press Enter. DOS copies the file and places the copy in the specified drive or directory.

Table 2.1 Sample COPY Commands

Command	What It Does
copy law.doc a:	Copies the file named LAW.DOC from the current directory to the disk in drive A
copy *.* b:	Copies all files in the current directory to the disk in drive B
copy c:\data*.doc a:	Copies all files in the DATA directory on drive C that have the extension .DOC to drive A
copy a:*.*	Copies all files on the disk in drive A to the current directory

Deleting Files

1. Change to the drive and directory that contain the file you want to delete.

2. Type del *filename.ext* and press Enter.

3. When DOS asks you to confirm the deletion, type y.

USING THE DOS SHELL If your version of DOS is 4.0 or later (for example, 4.01 or 5.0), it has a *shell program* that allows you to perform file management tasks more easily. (If you

INFORMATION
What's the asterisk (*) for? The asterisk is a *wild-card character* that stands in for any group of characters. *.* selects all files; *.doc selects only those files with the .DOC extension (the last three letters in the file's name).

CAUTION
Delete with caution. Be careful when deleting files. Although you may be able to recover accidentally deleted files, don't count on it.

are not sure which version of DOS you have, type **ver** at the DOS prompt and press Enter.)

Running the DOS Shell

1. Change to the drive and directory that contain your DOS files.

2. Type **dosshell** and press Enter. Figure 2.2 shows what the DOS shell looks like in version 5.0.

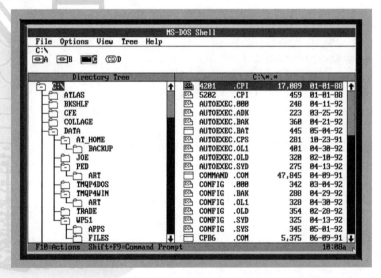

Figure 2.2 The DOS shell.

INSTALLING PROGRAMS

The first thing you should do when you get a program is write-protect the program disks and copy them.

The next step depends on whether or not the software comes with an installation program. If an installation program exists (usually called SETUP or INSTALL), you should run it before trying to use the application. In many cases, this installation program not only copies files but decompresses them, and also sets up the program to use your particular video display and printer.

19

If you can't find installation instructions in your documentation, you usually can get up and running in one of the following ways:

Installing a Program That Has an Installation Program

1. Insert your copy of the first program disk in the floppy disk drive.

2. Change to the drive that contains the program disk.

3. Type **dir /w** and press Enter. DOS displays a list of files on the disk.

4. Look at the list for files that end in .BAT, .EXE, or .COM. These are files that you can run. Of these files, look for files that start with INSTALL or INSTL or SETUP.

5. If you find such a program, type the name of the file, without the extension, and press Enter. For example, type **install** and press Enter. Then, go to step 6. If you don't find such a file, look at the directories of the other disks, and then skip ahead to the next set of steps.

6. Read and follow the messages on-screen to install the program.

Installing a Program That Does Not Have an Installation Program

1. Make a directory for storing the program files. Give the directory a name that will help you remember what's in the directory.

2. Change to the directory you just named; type **cd** and the name of the directory and press Enter.

3. Insert your copy of the first program disk into one of the floppy drives, A: or B:.

4. Type **copy a:*.*** or **copy b:*.*** and press Enter. DOS copies the files from the disk into the current directory.

5. If the program came on several disks, repeat steps 3 and 4 for each disk.

RUNNING PROGRAMS You will run programs in either of two ways: from floppy disks or from your hard disk. In either case, you type a command at the DOS prompt that tells DOS to run the program. The command is actually the name of one of the program files (the first part of the name). The documentation that came with the program tells you the command you must enter. If you don't have the documentation, refer to Chapter 4, "Surviving without Documentation." The following are general steps for running a program:

1. Change to the drive and directory that contain the program files.

2. Type the first part of the file's name. Omit the period and the extension. For example, to run Microsoft Windows, type `win`.

3. Press Enter.

SHUTTING DOWN To shut down the computer, don't just turn off the power. Doing so can cause the computer to forget things. Instead, follow this simple procedure:

1. If you've been working on anything, such as a letter, *save* your work in a file on disk and exit from the program.

2. Remove any disks from the floppy disk drive.

3. Turn off any devices that are connected to the computer, such as the printer, modem, and monitor.

4. Turn off the computer.

If you have a surge protector (a power strip that allows you to plug in several pieces of equipment), you can turn off everything at once by flipping the power switch on the strip. You should have a surge protector to prevent your computer from getting zapped by fluctuations in the power.

INFORMATION
If you are in the market for a more thorough explanation of DOS, and you like this book, get *At Home with MS-DOS*, by Paul McFedries. For a more comprehensive approach, look for *The Best Book of MS-DOS 5* by Alan Simpson.

3

TRANSFORMING YOUR COMPUTER SCREEN INTO A DESKTOP WITH MICROSOFT WINDOWS

In the last chapter, you saw how DOS lets you manage your disks and run programs. You may have noticed, however, that DOS is not very friendly; you'd better know what you're doing, because DOS isn't going to help. To make your computer easier to use, you can purchase a program called a graphical user interface (abbreviated GUI, pronounced Gooey). In the following sections, you learn the basics of using the most popular GUI program: Microsoft Windows.

GETTING GOOEY With Windows, instead of typing commands, you use a pointing device (usually a mouse) to select the command from a menu or to select a graphic symbol (*icon*) from the screen. If you have at least a 386SX with enough memory (2M), you can run several applications at the same time. Each application runs in its own *window*, as shown in Figure 3.1. You can arrange the windows in any manner, and you can size the windows for your convenience. As you can see, Windows transforms the computer screen into a desktop.

Figure 3.1 Each application runs in a window.

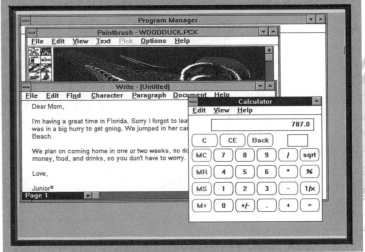

Before you can take advantage of Windows' ease-of-use, you have to start it from the DOS prompt. The following steps explain how to start Microsoft Windows.

Starting Microsoft Windows

1. Change to the drive that contains your Windows files. For example, type `c:` at the DOS prompt and press Enter.

2. Change to the directory that contains your Windows files. For example, if the name of the directory is WINDOWS, type `cd\windows` at the prompt and press Enter.

3. Type `win` and press Enter. DOS starts Windows. The Windows title screen appears for a few seconds, and then you see the screen shown in Figure 3.2.

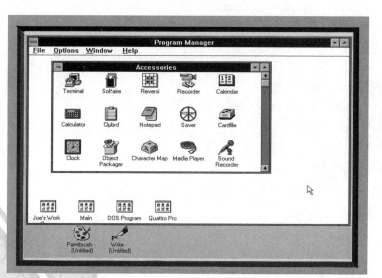

Figure 3.2 The Windows Program Manager.

A COURSE IN GOOEY ANATOMY As shown in Figure 3.2, the Windows user interface contains several unique elements that you won't see in DOS:

- *Title bar*. At the top of the window is a title bar containing the name of the window or program.

- *Program group windows and icons*. The Program Manager contains one or more windows, each containing a group of program-item icons.

- *Program-item icons*. Each program group window contains a collection of program-item icons. To run a program, you select its icon.

- *Minimize, Maximize, and Restore buttons*. These arrow buttons, in the upper right corner of each window, control window sizing. The Minimize button shrinks the window down to an icon. The Maximize button expands the window. The button then changes to a double-headed Restore button (not shown in Figure 3.2), which returns the window to its original size.

- *Control-menu box.* At the upper left corner of the active window is a Control-menu box. It looks like a minus sign. Selecting this box pulls down a menu which allows you to control the size and location of the window.

- *Pull-down menu bar.* This bar contains a list of the pull-down menus available in the program.

- *Mouse pointer.* Somewhere on the screen, a mouse pointer should appear (assuming you are using a mouse).

- *Scroll bars.* If a window contains more information than can be displayed in the window, a scroll bar appears at the edge of the window. The scroll arrows on each end of the scroll bar allow you to scroll slowly; the scroll box allows you to scroll more quickly.

- *Application icons.* If you run a program and then shrink its window down to the size of an icon, the icon is called an application icon. The program is still running, but it is running in the background. You can restore the application to window status by selecting its application icon.

USING A MOUSE To work most efficiently in Windows, you should use a mouse. You can press mouse buttons and move the mouse in various ways to change the way it acts:

- *Point* means to move the mouse pointer onto the specified item. The tip of the mouse pointer must be touching the item.

- *Click on an item* means to move the pointer onto the specified item and press the mouse button once. Unless specified otherwise, use the left mouse button.

- *Double-click on an item* means to move the pointer onto the specified item and quickly press and release the mouse button twice.

- *Drag* means to move the mouse pointer onto the specified item, hold down the mouse button, and move the mouse while holding down the button.

Figure 3.3 shows how to use the mouse to perform common Windows activities, including running applications and moving and resizing windows.

USING THE KEYBOARD Although Windows works best with a mouse, you can use your keyboard as well. The keyboard shortcuts listed in Table 3.1 explain how.

Table 3.1 Windows Keyboard Shortcuts

Press	To
Alt-Esc	Cycle through the application windows and icons
Ctrl-F6 (or Ctrl-Tab)	Cycle through program group icons and windows

continues

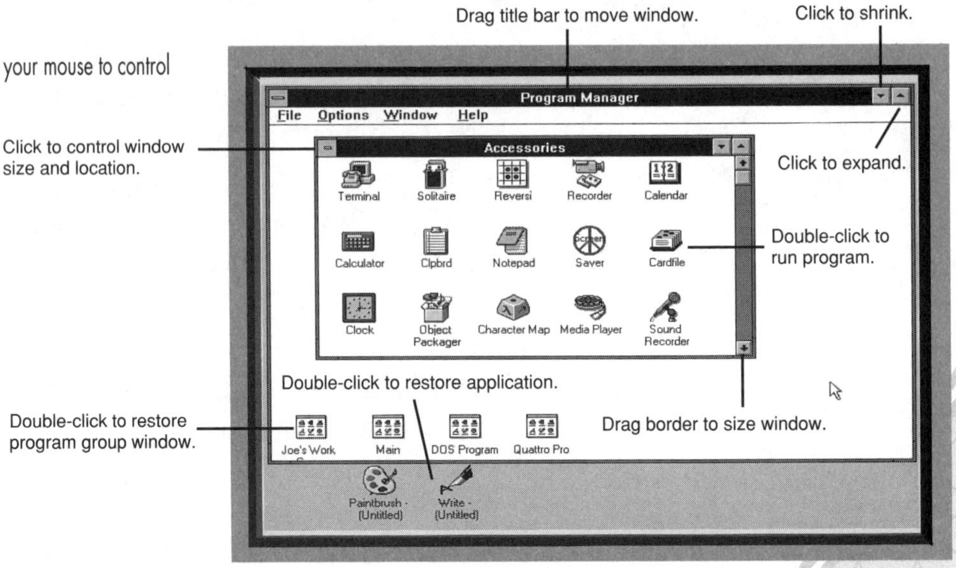

Figure 3.3 Use your mouse to control Windows.

Drag title bar to move window.

Click to shrink.

Click to control window size and location.

Accessories

Click to expand.

Double-click to run program.

Double-click to restore application.

Double-click to restore program group window.

Drag border to size window.

Table 3.1 Continued

Press	*To*
Alt-space bar	Open the Control menu for an application window or icon
Alt-hyphen	Open the Control menu for a program group window or icon
Arrow keys	Move from one icon to another in the active program group window
Alt (or F10)	Activate the pull-down menu bar
Alt-menu letter	Pull down a menu from the menu bar
Enter	Run the application whose icon is highlighted, or restore a window that has been reduced to an icon
Esc	Close a menu or dialog box

Press	To
Ctrl-Esc	View the task list, which allows you to switch to a different application
F1	Get help
Ctrl-F4	Minimize the selected program group window
Alt-F4	Exit the active application or exit Windows

NAVIGATING DIALOG BOXES Many times, when you enter a command in Windows, Windows displays a dialog box requesting additional information. For example, if you choose Properties from the File menu, you'll see the dialog box shown in Figure 3.4. Each dialog box contains one or more of the following elements:

- *Command buttons* such as OK and Cancel allow you to execute the command once you have made your selections in the dialog box. To press a command button, select it and press Enter.

- *List boxes* provide available choices. To activate a list, press Alt plus the underlined letter in the list's name or click inside the list box.

- *Drop-down lists* are similar to list boxes, but only one item in the list is shown. To see the rest of the items, click on the down arrow to the right of the list box, or press Alt plus the underlined letter in the list's name and then press the Down Arrow key.

- *Text boxes* allow you to type an entry. To activate a text box, click inside it or press Alt plus the underlined letter in the text box's name.

- *Check boxes* allow you to select one or more items in a group of options. For example, if you are styling text, you may select Bold and Italic to have the text appear in both bold and italic type.

- *Option buttons* are like check boxes, but you can select only one option button in a group.

Figure 3.4 A dialog box.

PROGRAMS THAT COME WITH WINDOWS In addition to providing you with a kinder and gentler interface, Windows comes with several useful programs (applications). Table 3.2 shows a list of commonly used programs.

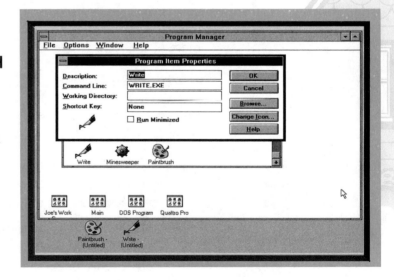

Chapter 3

30

Table 3.2 Microsoft Windows Programs

Program	What It Does
Write	Lets you type and print documents, such as letters and reports; offers several features that let you style the text
Notepad	Lets you jot down notes and create simple documents (does not offer features for styling text)
Cardfile	Acts as a Rolodex that sorts itself; helps you keep track of names, addresses, phone numbers, recipes, or any other information
Calculator	Works like a calculator you might keep on your desk, except you cannot misplace it
Clipboard	Serves as a temporary holding area for text or graphics that you cut or copy from a program; lets you then "paste" it somewhere else in the document or in some other document
Games	Provides you with the following games: Solitaire and Reversi (Windows 3.0); Solitaire and Minesweeper (Windows 3.1)
Clock	Shows you what time it is according to the clock inside your computer
Terminal	Works through a modem to connect with other computers that have modems
Macro Recorder	Lets you record and play back a set of recorded keystrokes that allow you to perform a task quickly

RUNNING PROGRAMS FROM WINDOWS When you install
Windows, the installation program creates icons for many

of your programs, so you can run each program by selecting its icon. You can run a program from Windows in two ways, depending on whether the program does or does not have an icon.

Running a Program That Has an Icon

1. Change to the window that contains the program's icon.

2. Double-click on the program's icon, or use the arrow keys to highlight it and press Enter.

Running a Program That Does Not Have an Icon

1. Press Alt-F or click on File in the Program Manager's pull-down menu.

2. Select Run.

3. Type a complete path to the directory in which the program's files are stored, followed by the name of the file that executes the program. For example, type
`c:\word5\word.exe`.

4. Press Enter or click on the OK button.

ANOTHER GOOEY PROGRAM Although Microsoft Windows is the most popular graphical user interface, it is not the only one. Another popular GUI program is GeoWorks. GeoWorks looks and behaves a lot like Windows. Some users consider it easier to use, but not as powerful as Windows.

4

SURVIVING WITHOUT DOCUMENTATION

Worst-case scenario—you get a program, and there's no documentation. You don't have any friends who know how to use the program, and the local bookstore doesn't have a book about this program. What do you do? The following sections provide some tactics for dealing with such situations. Although they won't work for all programs, they will work for most.

PRINT A LIST OF PROGRAM FILES To solve any mystery, you must use the information you have to find out what you don't know. In this case, the information you have consists of the names of the files that make up the program, and these names can tell you a lot. So the first thing you should do is print out the list of file names.

Printing a List of File Names

1. Change to the drive and directory that contain the program's files. (Refer to Chapter 2.)

2. Make sure your printer is turned on.

3. Type `dir > prn` and press Enter. DOS prints a directory listing containing the names of all files in the current drive and directory (see Figure 4.1).

```
              Volume in drive B is GWS
            Volume Serial Number is 12EB-2009
                 Directory of B:\

    GWS      EXE    176410 04-29-92    2:18p
    GWS      DOC    129796 11-07-91    3:28p
    GWSINSTL EXE     37458 11-07-91   11:31a
    GWSDRV   RES    107225 11-07-91    2:39p
    GWSPDR   RES     32044 08-11-91    6:08p
    GWS      RES    143239 11-07-91    3:35p
    EXAMPLE2 GIF     24576 01-01-80    3:36a
    EXAMPLE3 GIF     27878 08-25-91   10:52a
    RMOVER   EXE     19034 09-08-91    3:00p
    EXAMPLE1 IMG     62630 08-28-91    3:00p
    GWSSCN   RES     10523 09-05-91   10:07p
    VIEW-ME  IMG     21041 12-20-90    6:48p
           12 file(s)      791854 bytes

                      662528 bytes free
```

Figure 4.1 A directory of files on disk.

LOOK FOR A FILE WITH ZIP Many programs come with their files *compressed*, so they take up less disk space and fewer disks. A common program used to compress files is PKZIP. PKZIP works in either of two ways: it creates a ZIP file (a file with the extension .ZIP) that contains all the program files in a compressed format, or it creates a file with the .EXE extension that decompresses the files automatically

TIP

Zipper stuck? If you receive a file with a ZIP extension, you need a program called PKUNZIP.EXE to unzip it. It may be on the program disk.

(this is called a self-extracting ZIP file). The method for decompressing files depends on the method used to compress the files.

Decompressing a ZIP File

1. Copy the ZIP file and the file PKUNZIP.EXE to a directory on your hard disk.

2. Change to the drive and directory that contain the ZIP file.

3. Type `pkunzip` *`filename`*`.zip` (where *filename* is the name of the ZIP file) and press Enter. PKUNZIP decompresses the file.

4. Delete the ZIP file from your hard disk (type `del` *`filename`*`.zip`) and press Enter.

Decompressing an .EXE ZIP File

1. Copy the .EXE ZIP file to a directory on your hard disk.

2. Change to the drive and directory that contain the .EXE ZIP file.

3. Type the .EXE file's name without the .EXE extension, and press Enter. The files are decompressed in the current directory.

4. Delete the .EXE file from your hard disk (type `del` *`filename`*`.exe`) and press Enter.

LOOK FOR A TEXT FILE If you find a file called READNE.BAT, README.COM, README.EXE, or a similar name with the extension .BAT, .COM, or .EXE, you can run the program to display the documentation. To run the program, type its name at the DOS prompt and press Enter.

If you don't find one of those, look for a README text file, usually called READ.ME, README.TXT, README.DOC, or any file with the .DOC or .TXT extension. README files often contain information about installing and running the program. If you find such a file, take the following steps to display its contents:

Reading a Text File

1. Change to the disk and directory that contain the text file.

2. Type `type filename.ext | more` (where *file-name.ext* stands for the name of the text file). The command *type* tells DOS to "type" the contents of the file on-screen, and | *more* tells DOS to pause after displaying each screenful of information.

3. Press Enter. DOS displays the first screenful of information (see Figure 4.2).

4. Read the information, and then press any key to see the next screen.

5. Repeat step 4 until you are returned to the DOS prompt.

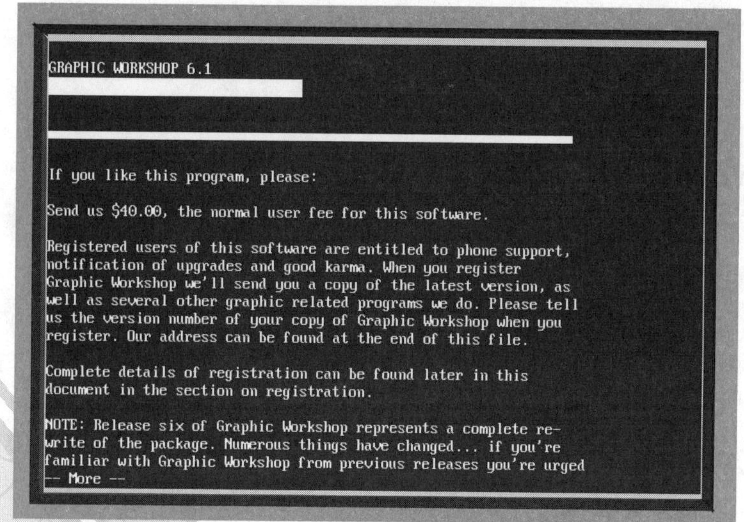

Figure 4.2 One screenful of information.

If you want to print the file, type the following command (all on one line), and press Enter (remember to substitute the actual file's name in place of *filename.ext*):

```
copy filename. ext > prn
```

LOOK FOR FILES THAT END IN .BAT, .COM, OR .EXE A

README file is nice, but it's not essential—you usually can get along without it. Keep in mind that your first goal is to get the program running, and that the three types of files that run a program have names that end in .BAT, .COM, and .EXE. So go back to your list of file names, and mark all the files that end in .BAT, .COM, or .EXE.

Now you can start narrowing down the list. First, look for .BAT files. Mark any batch file whose name appears to represent the program's name. For example, say you have a program called BlackDoom; look for names such as BD.BAT, BLACK.BAT, or BDOOM.BAT. Do the same for file names that end in .COM and .EXE.

Now you can try running the program. Use each promising file name, from most promising to least promising

(.BAT files first, .COM second, and .EXE third), until you hit on the right one.

Running a Program

1. Change to the drive and directory that contain the program files.

2. Type the first part of the file's name. Omit the period and the extension.

3. Press Enter. If the program started, you're all set. If not, go back to step 2 and try again.

THE PROGRAM IS RUNNING, NOW WHAT? Once you have a program up and running, your next concern is how to get around in the program. The technique for navigating in the program will vary depending on whether the program is *command-driven* or *menu-driven*. With command-driven programs, each command corresponds to a *function key* or a key combination, such as F5 or Ctrl-F1 or Shift-F3. With menu-driven programs, you can select commands from a pull-down menu.

MENU-DRIVEN? A PIECE OF CAKE If you start a program and a menu appears on-screen, you're in luck. To enter commands, you simply open a menu and select the command. You have only one initial problem—how to open a menu. Here are some techniques that work in a wide range of programs:

- In most programs (including all Windows programs), you can activate a menu by pressing Alt plus the highlighted letter or first letter in the menu's name. If that doesn't work, try pressing Esc or Ctrl.

- Look at the top or bottom of a screen for a message such as `Press Alt for menus` or `Right-click for menus`.

- Move the mouse pointer to the top of the screen and click the left button, the right button, or (if all else fails) both buttons at the same time.

- Once a menu is open, you usually can switch to the menu on the left or right by using the Left and Right arrow keys.

- To open a menu, either click on its name or press Alt plus the highlighted letter or the first letter in the menu's name.

- To choose an item from a menu, click on the item, or type the highlighted letter in the item's name, or use the arrow keys to highlight it and then press Enter.

LOOK AGAIN AT THE SCREEN

You'll often be surprised at the number of problems and mysteries you can solve by taking a step back and looking carefully at the screen. Many programs display a function key bar at the bottom of the screen that shows the commands you can enter. Simply press a function key to enter the designated command.

Figure 4.3 A message bar at the bottom of the screen.

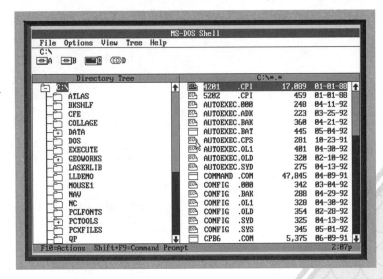

Other programs display a status line at the bottom of the screen that contains messages about what you can do next. For example, you might see the message **READY**, meaning you can start working. Or the message may tell you which key you need to press, as shown in Figure 4.3.

LOOK FOR HELP WITH F1 Just as 911 is a standard phone number to call in case of emergencies, the F1 key is used by most programs to display a Help screen. Try pressing the F1 key and see what happens. Many programs display a Help index that lists help with keystrokes. If this choice is available, choose it to find out which keys you need to press to enter commands.

If the Help screen contains a Print command, select this command to print the information you need. If a Print command is not available, make sure the help you need is displayed on-screen, and then press the Print Screen key. (You may have to hold down the Shift key while you press Print Screen to get it to work.) This sends everything on-screen to your printer. It's a messy way to print, but it gets you what you need.

TIP
If F1 doesn't work, try F3. Some programs (such as WordPerfect) assign the Help feature to the F3 key.

Chapter
4

> **TIP**
> **Tutorial through the Help system.** If you stumble upon a Help system in a program, the Help system may contain a tutorial, which you can run from within the Help system.

A BUILT-IN TUTOR? YOU'VE STRUCK GOLD Some programs come with a tutorial that leads you through the process of using the program's major features. Display a directory of the program's files and look for a file such as TUTOR.EXE, TUTOR.COM, LEARN.EXE, or LEARN.COM. If you find such a file, try running it.

WHEN ALL ELSE FAILS Okay, so you've tried everything and the screen still gives you a blank stare. Don't give up yet. Here are some final words of wisdom from our resident hacker, Faithe Wempen:

- *Watch the screen and press each function key.* Observe what each function key does, and take notes. Try each function key alone, and then in combination with Shift, Ctrl, and/or Alt.

- *If function keys don't work, try the other keys.* Start with the number keys, then the letter keys, each separately and in conjunction with Alt, Ctrl, and/or Shift, until you find something that changes the screen in some way.

- *Press the* Esc *key.* A menu or a message might appear telling you what to do next.

- *Click or click-and-hold the left mouse button on an item.* Many times, this will give you an explanation of the item or will call up a menu. If that doesn't work, try the *right* mouse button.

- *To exit, press* Esc, Ctrl-Esc, *or* Ctrl-Break. If none of these keys works, perform a *warm boot* as a last resort: Ctrl-Alt-Del.

USE COMMON SENSE Every suggestion in this chapter is built on common sense. You merely are looking for ways to find help, just as you look for help when you are lost; you try to find a person who has an intelligent face, or you look for a familiar landmark. Don't be afraid to try these various tactics. You won't hurt anything, and you probably will learn a great deal.

5

I JUST WANT TO TYPE A LETTER

I got the title for this chapter from my wife, Cecie. When I set up our fancy new 386SX, 16-megahertz, hundred-meg-hard-drive, two-megs-RAM, super-VGA, with-an-inkjet-printer computer that we paid three thousand bucks for, she looked at it and said, "I just want to type a letter." So much for trying to justify the expense. In this chapter, we will look at one of the most popular word processing programs on the market: WordPerfect 5.1.

PROCESSING WORDS?! Whoever came up with the idea of calling a program that lets you type letters a word processing program?

> "What are you doing, honey?"

> "Oh, just processing a few words."

. . . sort of like shredding carrots and purple cabbage for a salad.

So, what is a word processing program? It is a program that allows you to use your computer to type letters, create resumes, keep lists, address envelopes, and perform other tasks that you would perform using a typewriter.

Is that all? Well, not really. Most word processing programs can do a lot more, such as checking the spelling in your document and allowing you to paste pictures. But this chapter is for those of you who want to type a quick letter—no fancy stuff. So, if you want to see the fancy stuff, skip ahead to Chapter 6.

STARTING THE PROGRAM Whenever you want to use your computer to perform a task, you have to run an application first. In this case, you have to run a word processing program. You cannot simply start typing at the DOS prompt or in Windows. To learn how to run a DOS program, refer to Chapter 2. To run a Windows program, refer to Chapter 3.

WORKING WITH ELECTRONIC PAPER Most word processing programs start you out with a blank "sheet of paper" on-screen. The screen is not as long as a real sheet of paper, and it may be black instead of white, so you'll have to use your imagination. The program also displays a *cursor* or *insertion point*; anything you type is inserted at this point. When the cursor reaches the bottom of the screen, the program will move the "page" up, so you can continue typing. This is called *scrolling*.

People who move from a typewriter to a computer commonly run into the same problems. The following notes will help you avoid those problems:

- *You don't press Enter or Return at the end of every line*. The program wraps text automatically from one line to the next as you type. Press Enter or Return only to end a paragraph or to break a line.

- *You can't move down until there is something to move down to*. If you press the Down Arrow key on a blank screen, the cursor will not move down. If you want to move the cursor down on a blank screen, you have to press Enter to start a new paragraph.

- *Anything you type is inserted at the cursor*. If you move the cursor into the middle of a sentence and start typing, the text you type is inserted without replacing existing text. Surrounding text is adjusted to make room for the new text. You can switch to *overstrike mode* in which any text you type replaces existing text; the method for switching varies between programs.

- *Use the arrow keys or the mouse to move the cursor*. Many people try to move the cursor down by pressing Enter. This starts a new paragraph. Worse, some people try to move the cursor left by pressing the Backspace key. This moves the cursor all right, but it deletes any characters in the cursor's path. To move the cursor safely, use the arrow keys.

- *Just because something doesn't appear on-screen doesn't mean it is gone.* If you type more than a screenful of text, any text that does not fit in the screen is scrolled off the top of the screen. You can see the text by pressing PgUp or using the Up Arrow key to move the cursor to the top of the document.

- *Anything you type is saved only temporarily.* As you type, the text is stored in your computer's electronic memory. If you turn the computer off or quit the program, anything you type is lost. To save the text permanently, you must save it in a file on disk. Refer to the next section: "Play It Safe—Save Your Letter to Disk."

- *Delete to the right, backspace to the left.* To delete a character that the cursor is on or a character to the right of the cursor, press Del. To delete characters to the left of the cursor, press the Backspace key.

Once you've grasped the behavior of word processing programs, typing is easy—just do it. Figure 5.1 shows a letter typed in WordPerfect, a popular word processing program.

PLAY IT SAFE—SAVE YOUR LETTER TO DISK As you type, your letter is stored in your computer's electronic memory. If you turn off your computer, or if the power goes out, even

TIP

If your computer has several likely on/off buttons and none of them say "ON" or "OFF," don't panic. Instead, look for the symbols | (one) and 0 (zero). In the Never-Never-Land of computers, one means on and zero means off (don't ask).

TIP

The directory must exist. You cannot save a file to a directory that does not exist.

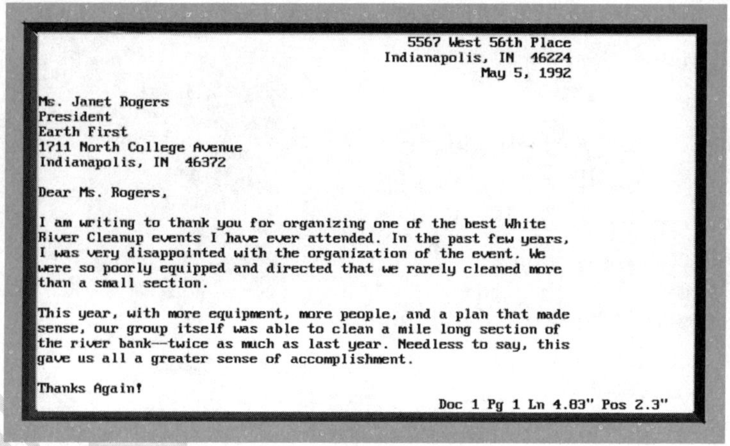

5567 West 56th Place
Indianapolis, IN 46224
May 5, 1992

Ms. Janet Rogers
President
Earth First
1711 North College Avenue
Indianapolis, IN 46372

Dear Ms. Rogers,

I am writing to thank you for organizing one of the best White River Cleanup events I have ever attended. In the past few years, I was very disappointed with the organization of the event. We were so poorly equipped and directed that we rarely cleaned more than a small section.

This year, with more equipment, more people, and a plan that made sense, our group itself was able to clean a mile long section of the river bank—twice as much as last year. Needless to say, this gave us all a greater sense of accomplishment.

Thanks Again!

Doc 1 Pg 1 Ln 4.83" Pos 2.3"

Figure 5.1 A letter typed in WordPerfect.

for a split second, your computer "forgets" your letter. You have to start over.

To prevent your letter from getting lost, save it to disk. The first time you save your file, you will have to name it and tell the program where to store it. Although the save operation differs from program to program, the following steps lead you through the basics:

1. If you are saving the file to a floppy disk, insert a disk in one of the floppy disk drives.
2. Enter the Save command. The procedure for entering the Save command differs from program to program. The program will ask you to specify a location and name for the file.
3. Type the path to the directory where you want the file saved, followed by the name of the file. For example, type:

   c:\data\letters\amanda.doc

TIP

File name restrictions. When naming a file, the name to the left of the period can be eight characters, and the extension to the right can be three characters. You cannot use any of the following characters:

" . / \ ? [ ] : * < > ¦ + ; , ?

If you are saving to a floppy disk drive, simply type **a:** or **b:** and then the file name. You don't need to specify a directory.

4. Press Enter. If you've already saved a file of the same name to the same directory, you will be warned that you are about to replace the existing file. If this happens, type a different name for the file.

Your letter is now saved to disk, and is safe. You can quit the program and turn off your computer without losing your letter. However, if you change the letter, you will have to save it again so the file on disk will contain the changes. When you save a file you already have saved, you don't have to name it; the program remembers the file's name.

PRINTING YOUR LETTER You can print your letter anytime it is displayed on-screen. It doesn't have to be saved to disk, and it doesn't even have to be finished. To print the letter, enter the Print command, which varies from program to program.

The program usually requests additional information, such as the print quality and the number of copies you want to print (see Figure 5.1). Supply the requested information, and then enter the command to start printing.

CLEARING THE SCREEN Once you are finished with your letter, save it and clear the screen so you can work on a different document. Clearing the screen removes the document from the screen and from your computer's random

> **TIP**
> **Menu-driven program?** If your word processing program has a pull-down menu bar, the Print command is usually on the File menu.

access memory (RAM). The procedure varies from program to program.

EDITING YOUR LETTER Before you can edit your letter, you must open the letter or retrieve it into the program you used to create the letter. This loads the letter into your computer's electronic memory (RAM), so you can work with it.

Opening a Document

1. Save any document that's displayed on-screen, and then clear the screen.

2. Enter the command for opening a document. (This command varies from program to program.) The program displays a message asking you to specify the name and location of the file.

3. Type a complete path to the drive and directory where the file is stored followed by the name of the file. For example, type:
   `c:\data\letters\amy.doc`.

4. Press Enter or enter the command to confirm that you want to open the file.

Once the letter is displayed on-screen, you can edit it. Use the following keys to move around the document:

- *Arrow keys.* Use the Up and Down Arrow keys to move the cursor up or down one line of text at a time. Use the Left and Right Arrow keys to move the cursor left or right one character at a time.

- *Ctrl-Arrow keys.* In most programs, you can move from word to word by holding down Ctrl while pressing the Left or Right Arrow key.

- *PgUp and PgDn keys.* Use the PgUp and PgDn keys to move up or down one screen at a time. This moves the cursor only one screen at a time; remember, a screen is shorter than an actual page.

- *Home and End keys.* The Home key usually moves the cursor to the beginning of a line. The End key moves the cursor to the end of a line.

OTHER WORD PROCESSING PROGRAMS Although Word-Perfect 5.1 is one of the most popular and most powerful word processing programs on the market, if you are just going to type letters, you don't need all that power. A less powerful, less complex program may be better for you, and there are several out there, including:

LetterPerfect

PC-Write

PFS: Write

Windows Write (included with Microsoft Windows)

GeoWrite (included with GeoWorks)

6

YOUR PERSONAL EDITOR

In Chapter 5, you saw how you can use word processing programs to write letters and perform other tasks that require typing. What you didn't learn is that there are additional tools that can make your writing clearer and more concise. In this chapter, we look at several writing tools that come with most word processing programs and two writing tools that don't: a dictionary (The American Heritage Dictionary) and a grammar checker (RightWriter).

ADVANCED WORD PROCESSING TOOLS In addition to letting you type, save, and edit letters, most word processing programs come with several advanced features to help you with your work:

- *Spell checker.* The spell checker compares each word in your document with a word in its dictionary. If it finds a word in your document that does not match a word in the dictionary, the spell checker lets you know (see Figure 6.1).

- *Thesaurus.* If you can't think of just the right word, the thesaurus may be able to help. You type the word you can think of and then look the word up in the thesaurus to view a list of synonyms (words that have the same meaning). See Figure 6.2.

- *Search and replace.* Say you write a training manual that explains how to make a widget. At the last minute, the company decides to call the part a *gadget* instead of a *widget*. You can use the search and replace feature to replace all occurrences of *widget* with *gadget*.

- *Graphics.* A program that supports graphics allows you to place a picture and/or lines on a page. Most word processing programs do not allow you to create the picture; you must create the picture using a graphics program and then bring it into your document.

- *Cut and paste.* With word processing programs, you can cut text and paste it somewhere else in the document. Most programs let you cut and paste between two or more documents.

- *Multiple windows.* With multiple windows, you can divide your screen into two or more windows and open a different document in each window. You then can switch between windows or cut and paste text from one window to the other.

INFORMATION

Define the word "dictionary." The dictionary in a word processing program contains a collection of words, but does not include definitions. It is used only to check the spelling of words.

- *Mail merge.* Have you ever gotten a letter from Ed McMahon, personally addressed to you? Well, Ed personalizes those form letters by using mail merge. He combines a form letter with a list of names and addresses to create a series of letters all saying the same thing to different people.

- *WYSIWYG or page preview.* WYSIWYG stands for What-You-See-Is-What-You-Get. This feature shows text on-screen approximately the way it will appear in print.

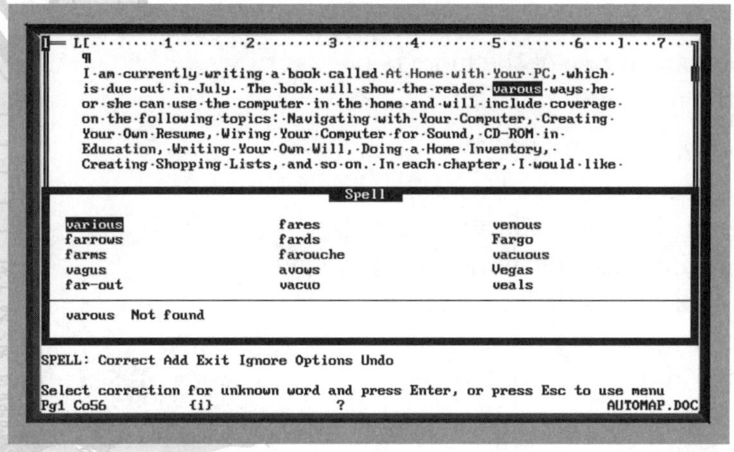

Figure 6.1 A spell checker in action.

```
L[········1·········2·········3·········4·········5·········6···]···7···
¶
I·am·currently·writing·a·book·called·At·Home·with·Your·PC,·which·
is·due·out·in·July.··The·book·will·show·the·reader·various·ways·he·
or·she·can·use·the·computer·in·the·home·and·will·include·coverage·
on·the·following·topics:·Navigating·with·Your·Computer,·Creating·
Your·Own·Resume,·Wiring·Your·Computer·for·Sound,·CD-ROM·in·
Education,·Writing·Your·Own·Will,·Doing·a·Home·Inventory,·
Creating·Shopping·Lists,·and·so·on.··In·each·chapter,·I·would·like·

                           Spell
various          fares             venous
farrows          fards             Fargo
farms            farouche          vacuous
vagus            avows             Vegas
far-out          vacuo             veals

varous   Not found

SPELL:  Correct  Add  Exit  Ignore  Options  Undo

Select correction for unknown word and press Enter, or press Esc to use menu
Pg1 Co56        {i}              ?                        AUTOMAP.DOC
```

Figure 6.2 A thesaurus helps you find the right word.

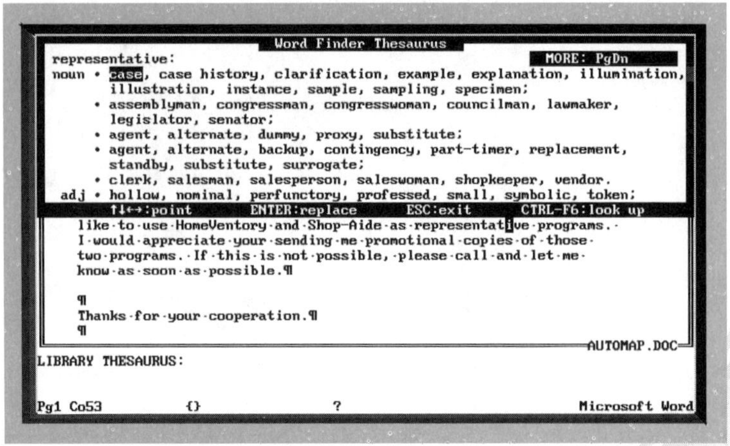

CHECKING YOUR GRAMMAR

If you overuse passive voice but you don't even know what passive voice is, if you can't make a subject and a verb agree, or if you wouldn't recognize a sentence fragment if one came up and bit you, consider getting a grammar checker. In this section, we look at one of the more popular grammar programs on the market: RightWriter.

54

Checking Your Document You can have RightWriter analyze your document word by word and sentence by sentence to point out possible weaknesses. The program acts like a spell checker; it stops on any questionable phrase and allows you to correct the problem or skip it (see Figure 6.3). The program is especially good at finding passive voice, overly long sentences, and subject-verb disagreement.

TIP

Shopper's tip. Whenever you shop for a writing tool such as a grammar checker, make sure the program is compatible (works) with your word processing program.

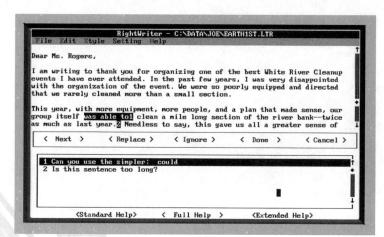

Figure 6.3 Correct errors as you go.

If you don't like going through your document phrase by phrase, you can have the program analyze a document and mark it up for you, just as a human editor might do. The program inserts comments in the document, which point out possible problem areas (see Figure 6.4).

Analyzing a Document for Readability If you're a bottom-line person, all you want to know about your document is whether the people you are writing for will understand it. You want to know if the document is appropriate for the reading level of your audience.

Most grammar checkers analyze your document for readability. The program determines the average number of words in each sentence and the average number of syllables in each word. It compares these averages against its standards to determine how complex the document is. The program then tells you the reading level required to understand the document.

```
                                    5525 West Mulberry
                                    Boulevard
                                    Indianapolis, Indiana
                                    46032
                                    May 8, 1992


       Ms. Helen Rogers
       President
       Carrier NewCorp, Inc.
       1277 West Open Field Drive
       Indianapolis, Indiana  46754

       Dear Ms. Rogers,

       I saw your ad in last Sunday's Indianapolis Star for a
       maintenance person, and I am interested<<*_ "am interest-
       ed" is passive voice.  Consider using the active voice.
       *>> in the position.<<*_ Would this sentence be clearer if
       it were split into two or more sentences? *>>

       Having worked for several manufacturing plants throughout
       Indiana, from 1985 till the present, I feel that I am very
       qualified for the position you currently<<*_ Consider
       replacing "currently" with the simpler "now" *>> have
       open, and I am interested<<*_ "am interested" is passive
       voice.  Consider using the active voice. *>> in it as
       well.<<*_ Would this sentence be clearer if it were split
       into two or more sentences? *>> In my most recent posi-
       tion, I was made<<*_ "was made" is passive voice.
       Consider using the active voice. *>> responsible for the
       upkeep of<<*_ Consider using a less wordy phrase than
       "responsible for the upkeep of" *>> several CNC machines,
       including a lathe, milling machine, and polisher.<<*_
       Would this sentence be clearer if it were split into two
       or more sentences? *>> In previous positions, I maintained
       and fixed various extruding machines and plastic injection
       molding machines, which has given me a wide variety of
       experiences.<<*_ Would this sentence be clearer if it were
       split into two or more sentences? *>>

       As you can see, I am highly qualified<<*_ "am highly qual-
       ified" is passive voice.  Consider using the active voice.
       *>> for the position you advertised for, and I would hope
       that we can arrange a time to meet for an interview.<<*_
       Would this sentence be clearer if it were split into two
       or more sentences? *>>

       Sincerely,



       Dave McFarin
```

Figure 6.4 A document with comments.

DON'T KNOW WHAT IT MEANS? LOOK IT UP Most word processing programs use a dictionary only for checking the spelling of words in a document. They don't provide meanings for the words. However, you can purchase a separate dictionary for your computer that lets you look up meanings. Computer dictionaries, such as *The American Heritage Dictionary*, offer several advantages over dictionaries that come in book form:

- *Ease of use.* Instead of flipping through a dictionary to find the meaning of a word, you simply type the word or highlight it in your document; the dictionary finds the meaning for you.

- *Help.* If you type or spell a word incorrectly, the dictionary provides a list of words that it thinks you are trying to look up. You then can select the correct spelling from the list.

- *Search for multiple words.* You have a picture of the word in your head: it's a large bird that eats fish, but you can't think of its name. To find the word, you type `large AND bird AND fish` and press Enter. The program displays a list of birds that are large and eat fish: kingfisher, osprey, and pelican.

- *Paste.* If you look up a word in the dictionary's thesaurus, you can paste the word from the thesaurus into your document. You don't waste time typing the word, and you don't have to worry about typing the word correctly.

OTHER WRITING TOOLS Writing tools have become big business. One company (WordStar, which publishes *The American Heritage Dictionary*, which we just looked at) has a collection of several useful writing tools, including the following gems:

- *Correct Letters.* This tool contains several prewritten business letters for all occasions. You enter the inside address and your return address, and modify the letter however you wish, or send it as is.

- *Correct Quotes.* If you're one of those people who likes to throw quotes around, this helps ensure that you get the quote right and know the name of the person you are quoting.

- *Lexica.* If you have to translate your documents from English to French, German, Spanish, or Dutch, Lexica can help. Although it cannot perform the translation for you, it does help you look up vocabulary you are unfamiliar with.

With these writing tools and your own innate talent, you'll be well on your way to becoming an erudite and productive writer. (I found "erudite" in my thesaurus.)

7

CREATING PROFESSIONAL RESUMES AND COVER LETTERS

The job of looking for a job is usually more difficult than the job you eventually find. You must create a unique resume, locate potential job openings, write interesting cover letters, and keep everything organized. The good news is that your computer can help. In this chapter, we look at a program that helps you in every aspect of your search—PFS: Resume and Job Search Pro.

CREATING THE RESUME—IT'S AS SIMPLE AS FILLING IN THE BLANKS If you have a professional resume service design your resume, its representative will give you a form to fill out. You supply your name, address, and phone number; the type of job you are looking for; and your experience, qualifications, and education. The service then plugs the information into a template and churns out a resume—for a modest cost of fifty to a hundred bucks. When you get your fancy new resume home, you realize that you will

never be able to create a matching cover letter and envelope or customize the resume for different jobs.

With PFS: Resume and Job Search Pro, you get rid of the
middleman, you get matching resumes and cover letters,
and you can create custom resumes for special jobs. To
create a resume, open the Resume menu and choose New
Resume. The program displays several types of resumes, as
shown in Figure 7.1; select the type that most closely
matches the type of job for which you are applying.

TIP

Sample resumes. To view
sample resumes, you can
choose Load Resume from
the Resume menu, press
F3, and then select a
resume from the list.

Figure 7.1 Select a type of resume.

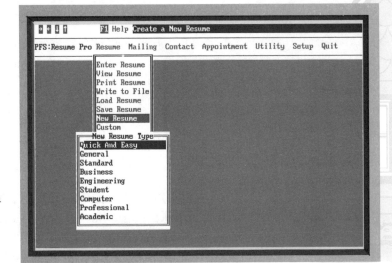

The program then displays
the form shown in Fig-
ure 7.2, requesting the
following information:

- *Name, address,
  and phone number.*
  If you have two
  addresses, you can
  enter both. Or
  you can enter a
  complete home
  address and phone
  number as the first entry and your phone number
  at work as the second entry.

- *Titles for each section of your resume.* Most resumes
  are broken down into sections, such as Career

TIP
Previewing the resume.
You can see how your
resume will appear in print,
without actually printing it,
by pressing the F9 key.

Objective, Experience, Education, and References. In the Title box, you enter the title of each section as you want it to appear on the resume.

- *Categories for each style you want to use.* In the Category box to the right of the Title box are several styles for displaying the information that appears under each title.

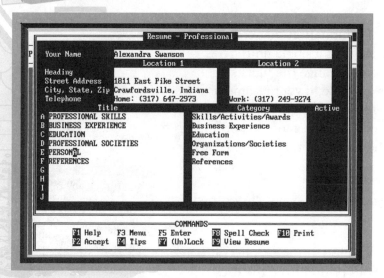

Figure 7.2 Type the information.

CUSTOMIZING YOUR RESUME

Once you have created a basic resume, you can go back and customize it by choosing Custom from the Resume menu and changing the following formats:

- *Fonts.* A font is a set of characters that have the same design and size. You can change the font for headings, sub-headings, and body text.

- *Page*. You can set the top, bottom, left, and right margins, the page length, and the distance that text is indented from the left edge of the page. This is useful if your resume is less than a page long; you can fiddle with the margins to make it look longer.

- *Style*. You can choose how you want certain elements printed on the page. For example, you can have your name centered or pushed flush against the left margin.

- *Layout*. Each block of information that corresponds to a title is treated as a single unit. The Layout option lets you rearrange the blocks of information. So, for example, if your resume lists your job experience first, and you are applying for a job in which your education is more important, you can rearrange the blocks so that your education appears first.

PRINTING THE RESUME Once you've created and customized your resume, the rest is easy:

1. Open the Setup menu and select Printer. A list of printers appears. Select your printer from the list. (You have to set up the printer only the first time you print.)

2. Open the Resume menu and select Print Resume. A dialog box appears, as shown in Figure 7.3. Change any of the options as desired.

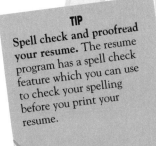

TIP
Spell check and proofread your resume. The resume program has a spell check feature which you can use to check your spelling before you print your resume.

3. Press F2 to start printing.

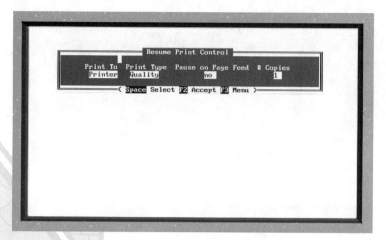

Figure 7.3 You can control the quality of the printout.

COLLECTING JOB CONTACTS

Once you have a resume, you need somewhere to send it. Scan the newspapers every day for job leads, talk to other people in your field, and make a list of all your contacts. PFS: Resume and Job Search Pro can help you keep a list of job contacts (see Figure 7.4). You then can have information inserted from your list into the cover letters you create later.

CREATING A MATCHING COVER LETTER A cover letter is as important as your resume. You want a letter that compels your prospective employer to read the resume. If you have any information about the company and the job opening, be sure to read it before you start writing your letter. Then make sure your letter tells exactly how your experience and talents make you the best person for this job.

To write the letter, use the word processor that's part of Resume and Job Search Pro. To use the word processor, open the Mailing menu and select Word Processor.

TIP
Get names of real people. When making a list of job contacts, try to get the names of real people by calling the company.

63

Figure 7.4 Record your job prospects.

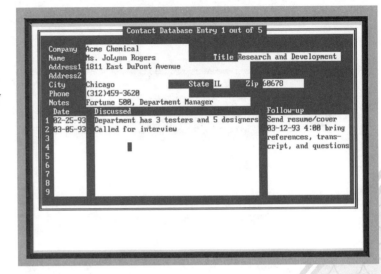

INSERTING CONTACT INFORMATION INTO YOUR COVER LETTER

If you already have entered information for your job contacts, you don't have to retype the information in your cover letter. Instead, you can have the program merge your letter with the contact information by inserting merge codes in the letter, as shown in Figure 7.5. The program prints the letter(s), inserting information from the contact list into each one.

MAKING A MATCHING ENVELOPE

Now that you have a cover letter and resume, you need an envelope to put them in. With Resume and Job Search Pro, you print an envelope by filling out the form shown in Figure 7.6.

DON'T BE LATE FOR THAT IMPORTANT MEETING

PFS: Resume and Job Search Pro also features a calendar that you can use to keep track of your appointments. When you select Appointment from the menu bar, the program displays a calendar for the current month. If you select a day in that month, the screen shown in Figure 7.7 appears. You can then enter information about the appointment.

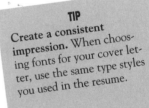

TIP
Create a consistent impression. When choosing fonts for your cover letter, use the same type styles you used in the resume.

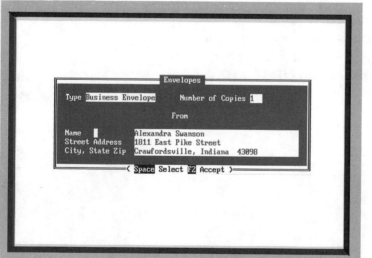

```
Memory: 56k          Layout: Left         Indent: None      ESC MENU  F1 HELP
1: Line 27 of Page   1   Style: Normal                      ▲ ▼ ◄ ►    Insert
Typeface:  1: Dixon                       12 pt    Spacing: 1.00   Hyphen: Off
<......█.2.....¦...3...¦...4.¦........¦...6....¦...>.........8......R1
                                  Alexandra Blodgett
                                  Chicago, Illinois, 60658
                                  May 15, 1992

@m 2
@m 3
@m 1
@m 4
@m 5
@m 9


Dear @m 10:

I am writing in response to the sales position advertised in the May 13, 1992
issue of The Chicago Tribune.  As the enclosed resume shows, I am well-
qualified for the position. I am fluent in Spanish, English, and Japanese; I hav
over five years experience in corporate sales; and I am dedicated to continued
improvement.

Currently,█I am employed by XYZ Co. as the Corporate Sales Director.  By
```

Figure 7.5 Merge codes pull in information.

To find out about upcoming appointments, type the number of days you want to be notified in advance. The next time you select Appointment, choose Yes to check for any upcoming meetings.

Figure 7.6 You can print matching envelopes.

OTHER RESUME PROGRAMS

Although there are other resume programs on the market, I haven't seen any that are as complete and well thought-out as Resume and Job Search Pro. Most of the resume programs I looked at

Figure 7.7 Keep track of your appointments.

```
                                 Item 4 out of 9
  Date 05-29-92   Name Ms. Sylvia Beanmaster

  Type Interview          Reminder Days 2

  Time      Description
  4:30      Interview with Scott Cook (Research and Development) and
            Cherri Rogers (Program Manager), bring references,
            transcript, samples of work



                            COMMANDS
        ESC Quit    F2 Update   F5 New    F7 Print   PgUp Previous
        F1  Help    F3 Select   F6 Erase  F8 List    PgDn Next
```

supply several sample resumes that you can edit and very few type styles to choose from.

Of course, if you have a word processing program, you can use it to create your resume. But again, because these programs are not designed specifically for writing resumes and managing your job search, you have to spend a lot more time fiddling with your resume to get it just right. And when you are in a hurry to get your resume in the mail, time is something you don't have much of!

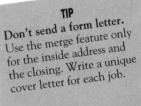

TIP
Don't send a form letter.
Use the merge feature only for the inside address and the closing. Write a unique cover letter for each job.

8

DON'T BE LATE: KEEP AN ON-SCREEN CALENDAR

Wouldn't it be nice to have your own personal secretary? This person would follow you around and keep track of all your appointments; let you know of all upcoming appointments and of any scheduling conflicts; tell you where you had to be, when you had to be there, and what you needed to bring; and remind you of all your relatives' birthdays and anniversaries. If you can't afford to hire such a person, consider getting a calendar program for your computer. In this chapter, we look at two such calendars: OnTime and The Far Side Calendar for Windows.

WHY PUT A CALENDAR ON A COMPUTER? In our house, we used to keep dates in several different places. We had a birthday and anniversary list stuck on one bulletin board. Our kids' school calendars were tacked up on another bulletin board. My wife and I each had our own pocket calendars. And we had a communal wall calendar to keep us all informed of everyone else's schedule. If that wasn't enough, I had a home maintenance schedule floating around in my head.

This system (if you can call it a system) was anything but efficient. We rarely looked at the birthday and anniversary list, as our friends and relatives can attest. If my wife or I forgot to transfer dates from our pocket calendars or from our kids' calendars to the communal calendar, we ran into scheduling conflicts. And I rarely did things when I was supposed to.

As you will see in this chapter, a computer calendar can help solve many of these problems.

KEEPING THE CALENDAR AT YOUR FINGERTIPS Most computer calendars run in either of two ways: as *stand-alone* programs or as *memory-resident* programs. As a stand-alone program, a calendar is just like any other calendar—you enter your appointments for each day, and then look at the calendar to find out about appointments and things you must do.

In memory-resident mode, the calendar becomes much more powerful. It runs in the background while you work with other programs. If someone calls to make a date, you press a *hot-key* (for example, Ctrl-Alt) for instant access to your calendar. If you turn on the alarm for an appointment, the calendar beeps and displays a message to inform you of any upcoming appointments (see Figure 8.1).

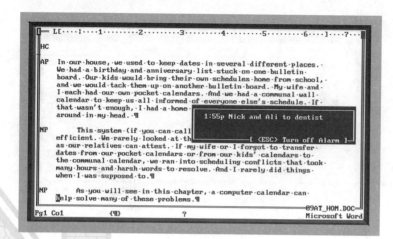

Figure 8.1 Keep informed of upcoming appointments.

Within the figure:
```
In our house, we used to keep dates in several different places.
We had a birthday and anniversary list stuck on one bulletin
board. Our kids would bring their own schedules home from school,
and we would tack them up on another bulletin board. My wife and
I each had our own pocket calendars. And we had a communal wall
calendar to keep us all informed of everyone else's schedule. If
that wasn't enough, I had a home
around in my head. ¶
```
```
1:55p Nick and Ali to dentist

[ <ESC> Turn off Alarm ]
```
```
     This system (if you can call
efficient. We rarely looked at th
as our relatives can attest. If my wife or I forgot to transfer
dates from our pocket calendars or from our kids' calendars to
the communal calendar, we ran into scheduling conflicts that took
many hours and harsh words to resolve. And I rarely did things
when I was supposed to. ¶
```
```
     As you will see in this chapter, a computer calendar can
help solve many of these problems. ¶
```
```
Pg1 Co1        {¶}              ?              09AT_HOM.DOC
                                              Microsoft Word
```

MAKING APPOINTMENTS

Before you can take advantage of the computer calendar, you must enter the necessary information for each appointment. In most calendar programs, you enter an appointment by selecting the date and time of the appointment and entering a command to add an appointment to the calendar. The program then displays a dialog box such as the one shown at the bottom of Figure 8.2, allowing you to enter the necessary information.

KEEPING TRACK OF BIRTHDAYS, WEDDINGS, AND ANNIVERSARIES If you are one of those people who always misses the birthdays and anniversaries of your friends and relatives, consider recording those special dates on your calendar. You record the occasion once, and the program takes care of the entry for each subsequent year.

KEEPING A HOME MAINTENANCE SCHEDULE When you buy your own home, you get a whole new set of responsibilities. You have a furnace and air conditioner to maintain, a lawn that needs to be fertilized, windows to be washed, gutters to be cleaned, and so on. In the hustle and bustle

TIP
First in, last out. With memory-resident programs, the first program you run should be the last program you remove from memory. Remember the order in which you load your programs.

Figure 8.2 Fill in the blanks.

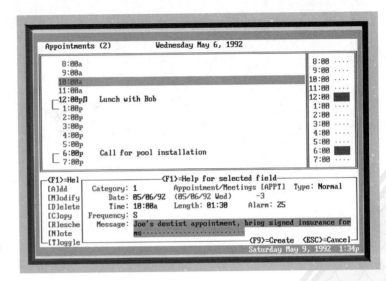

of everyday life, it's easy to forget these things.

To help you remember what you have to do around the house—and when—you can create a home maintenance schedule using a calendar program. In OnTime, you can create such a maintenance schedule by creating a To-Do list. You can even repeat the To-Do entry on a regular basis. For example, if you need to change the air filter in your furnace every month, you can have the entry repeated on a monthly basis.

SEARCHING THROUGH YOUR CALENDAR OnTime offers a unique feature that lets you search your calendar for important dates. For example, say you want a list of items dealing with birthdays:

1. Enter the command to perform a search.

2. Type `:birthday` and press Enter. (The colon (:) tells the program that the word can be anywhere in the message.) OnTime searches through all the appointments, birthday and anniversary entries, and To-Do

TIP
Help! If you need to fill in a blank, and you don't know what your options are, move the cursor to the blank (usually by pressing the Tab key), and press the program's Help key (usually F1).

lists to find the word `birthday` and displays a list of corresponding entries.

3. Type `P` to print out a list of the entries.

ONTIME FOR WINDOWS—A PROGRAM WITH A DIFFERENT LOOK AND FEEL If you have Microsoft Windows, you should consider getting the Windows version of OnTime instead of the DOS version. OnTime for Windows displays a calendar that is much more logical to use. It is shown in Figure 8.3.

HUMOROUS CALENDARS Up to this point, we've looked at a serious calendar. If you prefer a light-hearted calendar, and if you have Microsoft Windows, take a look at The Far Side calendar. When you start this calendar, you see a Far Side cartoon, just as you might see on a desktop calendar (see Figure 8.4). You can then click on one of the buttons at the bottom of the Far Side window to view your calendar one day at a time (see Figure 8.5). You can also view a week, a month, or an entire year. Although The Far Side calendar is humorous, it does have an alarm feature, animated reminders, and other advanced features; it's not just a toy.

Now that you have your own personal secretary, you have no more excuses for missing important dates or being late to meetings. Of course, you don't have to tell anyone you have a calendar program.

INFORMATION
Automatic rollover. Many calendars offer an automatic rollover feature that keeps an item on the To-Do list until you delete it.

Figure 8.3 OnTime for Windows.

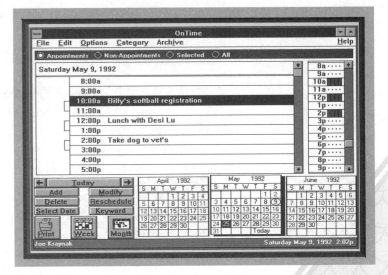

Figure 8.4 A cartoon from the Far Side calendar.

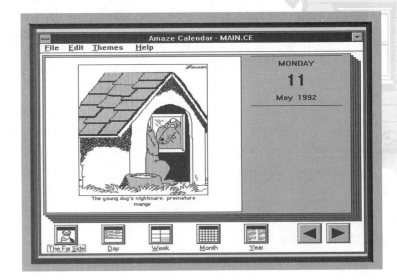

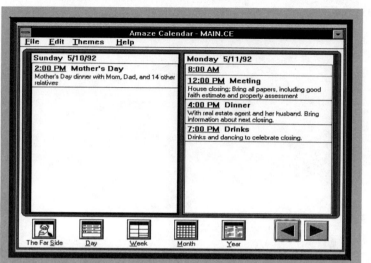

Figure 8.5 The Far Side calendar's practical side.

9
TAKE CONTROL OF YOUR LIFE

Life is complicated. There are doctors to call, homes and cars to be repaired, and pizzas to order. You have friends and relatives to keep track of, job leads you may need or may never need, business associates to keep in touch with, and maybe even a home business to keep organized. In this era of information overload, you need all the help you can get. In this chapter, we look at a program that can help you get organized: Info Select.

AN ORGANIZED STACK OF NOTES Info Select is a unique program in that it allows you to enter information in any order or in no order. If you are used to keeping lists, you can continue keeping lists. If you like to write notes on Post-Its, you can continue doing that. If you use a Rolodex, you can use the program as an electronic Rolodex. In short, you can be as disorganized as you want—Info Select will take care of finding the information later.

NAMES, ADDRESSES, AND PHONE NUMBERS AT YOUR
FINGERTIPS Most people keep an address book that contains the names, addresses, and phone numbers of their friends and relatives. But what do you do with the phone numbers you get from other people and places? For example, say an insurance representative gives you a business card, or you find a pizza joint you really like, or each member of your family goes to a different doctor.

With most people, these phone numbers and contacts get stuck on a bulletin board or stuffed in a basket or a purse, where they are destined to get lost. With Info Select, you can enter all the names, addresses, phone numbers, and any other information, as shown in Figure 9.1. The information is in one central location, and the program will help you find it at the press of a key.

76

INFORMATION
Free-form database. Info Select is often referred to as a free-form database. That is, the database does not require you to enter the information in any set pattern.

Figure 9.1 Enter the information in one place.

Finding a Name, Address, or Phone
Number So you've entered all the names, addresses, and phone numbers in no particular order. You have hundreds of windows, most of which you can't even see. How is this disorganized system better than the one you had? The answer is that the program will fetch the information for you.

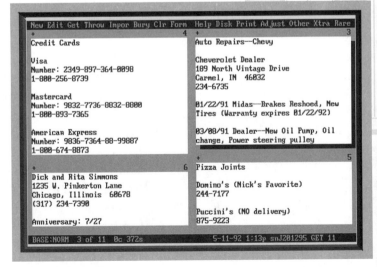

Here's how easy it is in Info Select:

1. Type G for Get.

2. Start typing any word, number, or other piece of information that is contained in the entry you want to find. (See Figure 9.2.)

3. Press Enter. Info Select displays all the entries that contain the text you typed.

Having Info Select Dial a Phone Number If your computer is connected to a modem, you can have Info Select dial phone numbers for you. Info Select can store many more phone numbers than any programmable phone on the market. With Info Select, dialing numbers is easy:

1. Display the entry that contains the phone number you want to dial.

2. Type O for Other and O for Outdial. Info Select moves to the first phone number it finds. To move to the next phone number, press the Down Arrow key.

3. When you are at the number you want to dial, type O or press Enter. Info Select starts dialing the number.

4. Depending on your modem, pick up the phone when Info Select starts dialing or when the other person answers. (Refer to your modem documentation.)

Figure 9.2 Type a word to look for at the bottom of the screen.

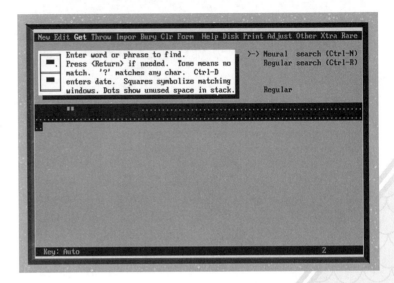

Gentle Reminders In addition to helping you organize all the information in your life, Info Select can remind you of important dates. You simply mark the date with a double-asterisk (**). When you start Info Select on the date marked, the program displays the entire entry that contains the marked date.

KEEPING TRACK OF HOME AND AUTO REPAIRS This is a true story. One day, I took my car in to the dealer because it was leaking oil. The dealer said that the car needed a new oil pump. Dollar signs flashed across my mind, I said OK, and I hung up.

Then, I started thinking that about six months earlier, one of our cars had the oil pump replaced. I couldn't remember which car, and I wasn't about to search through the repair bills we keep in the glove compartment of each car. I hot-keyed into Info Select (Alt-J), typed **G** for Get, and typed `oil pump`. The screen shown in Figure 9.3 appeared. I called the dealer and explained the situation. The free oil pump paid for Info Select and for several pizzas.

Figure 9.3 Keep track of your repair bills.

```
New Edit Get Throw Impor Bury Clr Form  Help Disk Print Adjust Other Xtra Rare
                                        4
Auto Repairs--Chevy

Cheverolet Dealer
189 North Vintage Drive
Carmel, IN  46032
234-6735

01/22/91 Midas--Brakes Reshoed, New
Tires (Warranty expires 01/22/92)

03/08/91 Dealer--New Oil Pump, Oil
change, Power steering pulley

06/23/91 Sears--New fuel pump

08/13/91 Midas--New muffler (1-year
warranty)

11/12/91 Dealer--Air filter and oil
change. Tightened oil pan.

BASE:NORM  12 of 12  2c 372s          5-11-92 1:20p snJ201295 GET 1
```

OTHER USES FOR INFO SELECT

Although Info Select is especially useful for creating an address book, it is flexible enough to be used for many other tasks as well:

- *Wedding plans.* You can keep a list of the people to be invited, the name and phone number of the dress shop and flower shop, a list of caterers and their price quotes, and the photographer's name and phone number.

- *Home renovations.* You can make a list of plumbers, electricians, and carpenters to call for quotes, record the information for each quote, and use Info Select to compare the information. You then can record dates and times to coordinate the work of all those involved.

- *To-Do lists.* You can keep a list of things you must do in the order in which you want them done. The To-Do list will help you stick to your schedule and get everything done on time.

TIP

Repair services. Use Info Select to keep track of the names and phone numbers of the repair services you commonly use for your home and car.

Chapter 9

79

- *Birthday and anniversary lists.* You can keep a list of your friends' and relatives' birthdays and anniversaries. With Info Select's Tickler feature, you can have the program notify you in time to get a card in the mail.

- *Credit card security.* If you have several credit cards, you can keep a list of the cards in case your wallet or purse gets stolen. List the name of the credit card, the credit card number, and the phone number to call if the card gets stolen. If you have a modem, you can have Info Select dial each number for you.

OTHER WAYS TO MANAGE INFORMATION Info Select is specially designed to help you manage all the information in your life. One advantage of this program is that it runs in the background—you can work in another program and switch to Info Select whenever you need it by using the hot-key (Alt-J). But there are other programs on the market that help you manage information. For example, if you have Microsoft Windows or GeoWorks, you already have a card file that you can use to create an address book (see Figure 9.4). Likewise, you can use a different database program, a spreadsheet program, or even a word processing program for storing and finding information.

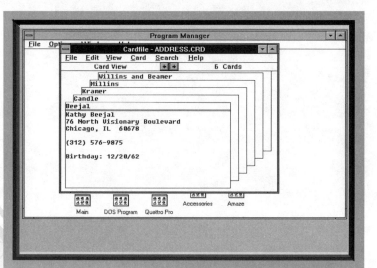

Figure 9.4 Microsoft Windows comes with a card file.

So why use Info Select? Because Info Select lets you enter information in any form and keeps a variety of information at your fingertips. With any of the other systems discussed here, you would spend a lot more time trying to figure out how to enter the information in an organized manner and how to find the information once you entered it.

10

TAKING CARE OF YOURSELF AND YOUR FAMILY

Doctors are no longer solely responsible for keeping us healthy. Now, the responsibility for our health rests on our own shoulders. We are expected to watch our diets, not smoke, avoid excessive drinking, and exercise regularly. Darn! Due to this new responsibility, we want to know what's really going into our bodies and what's going on when our bodies get sick. In this chapter, we look at two programs: one that helps you plan your diet (Health and Diet Pro) and one that helps you understand what's going on when you or a member of your family gets sick (Home Medical Advisor).

PLANNING A HEALTHY DIET Back in the not-so-old days, diet planning was simply a matter of counting calories in order to lose weight. Nowadays, diet planning is much more complex, because we have come to realize that not all calories are created equal. We have calories from protein, calories from fat, and calories from carbohydrates. And as if that's not enough, we also have to keep track of how much sodium, cholesterol, calcium, iron, and other stuff is going into our bodies.

Health and Diet Pro helps you keep track of all this vital information by offering the following features:

- *Information on over 3,000 foods*, including foods you would get at many fast-food restaurants and in the frozen food section of your grocery store. The program lists the type of food and the number of calories from fat, protein, and carbohydrates; the amount of fiber and cholesterol; and the amount of sodium, calcium, and iron. You can edit the list to add foods that are not included.

- *Food exchange values* for each of the foods listed.

- A *meal-planner system* that allows you to select various items from the food list and then tallies all the measurements to provide the total amounts for the meal.

- A *goal-setting feature* that allows you to set your own weight goal. The program determines the number of calories you should consume to reach the goal and breaks down the calorie count into calories from protein, fat, and carbohydrates. The program also makes adjustments for your level of activity and the various exercises you perform.

INFORMATION

Percents or calories? Health and Diet Pro determines the percentage of fat in terms of calories, not weight, giving you a more accurate and meaningful measurement.

- *Instant feedback* that shows how close you are to reaching your goal for the day. The program can show this information in a chart or on a graph.

- A *recipe maker* that lets you experiment with your recipes to determine how to cook healthier meals.

- A *standard meal feature* that allows you to save the information for a meal you commonly eat. For example, if you always have yogurt, a banana, and a glass of skim milk for breakfast, you can save the three foods as a standard meal and use it as your breakfast for each day.

SETTING DIET GOALS To set your goals, enter your name, sex, age, weight, level of activity during the day, number of pounds you want to gain or lose each week, and any exercises you regularly perform. The program tells you how many calories you need each day and breaks them down into calories from protein, fat, and carbohydrates (see Figure 10.1). It also recommends the amount of sodium, fiber, cholesterol, iron, and calcium you should consume each day.

PLANNING YOUR MEALS The central feature of Health and Diet Pro is the meal planner. When you choose to plan a meal, the program displays a calendar which allows you to select the day for which you want to plan your meals. You select a day and then tell the program what you want to eat for breakfast, lunch, dinner, and snacks. To plan a meal, select foods from the food list (which contains 3,000

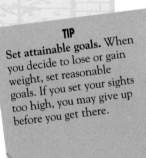

TIP
Set attainable goals. When you decide to lose or gain weight, set reasonable goals. If you set your sights too high, you may give up before you get there.

Figure 10.1 What you need to eat to reach your goal.

foods) and specify how many servings of each food you plan on eating.

Figure 10.2 shows a sample meal for Slim Jim Pickins. Slim plans on eating a bacon, lettuce, and tomato club sandwich for break- fast. As you can see, the program displays the daily goal for protein, carbohydrates, fat, and so on; the amount this meal contributes to each measurement; and the remaining amount needed for the day. If Slim wants to see the information displayed in a graph, he can press the F3 key.

ADDING FOODS TO THE FOOD LISTS Although the food list contains a wide variety of foods, it cannot cover every food you might encounter. But don't worry, Health and Diet Pro lets you edit the food list. You can delete any foods you never eat, add foods that you commonly eat, or change the information for a food that's already on the list.

EXPERIMENTING WITH RECIPES If you pick up a prepared meal from the frozen food section in the grocery, deter- mining food value is easy; you just look at the box. But when you actually prepare a meal using your own recipe,

The screen in Figure 10.1 shows:

People	Records	Reports	Utilities	Exit

Goals for: Slim Jim Pickins   Calories

Statistic		Per day
Calories		3563.43
Carbohydrates	(gm)	534.51
Protein	(gm)	133.63
Fat:Saturated	(gm)	32.99
Mono-Unsat	(gm)	32.99
Poly-Unsat	(gm)	32.99
Total	(gm)	98.98
Cholesterol	(mg)	250.00
Sodium	(mg)	1000.00
Fiber	(gm)	30.00
Iron		10.00
Calcium		1000.00

Press ↵ to edit

Calories are a measure of the energy contained in a food. You can think of them as the fuel which you need for your body to do work and to maintain body heat.

Like fuel, if you add more than you burn your storage tanks begin to fill, (you add weight). If you burn more than you add, then your storage tanks begin to empty, (you lose weight).

Use F7 and F8 to scroll text.

F1 Help	F3 Calendar	F5 Edit FEV's	F7 Scroll Up	F9 Edit
F2 Tables	F4 Day Planner	F6	F8 Scroll Dn	F10 Done

```
Who:
Slim Jim Pickins
Meal:                    Date:            Daily Statistics: Nutrient Values
  Breakfast             06/04/92
                                                    Daily      This     Remaining
                                          Stats      Goal      Meal      for day
% Calories from Fat:
    46 % today    46 % this meal       Calories   3774.00    660.00     3114.00
                                        Protein     188.70     34.00      154.70
                                        Cholest     250.00     64.00      186.00
Food                          # Svgs    Carbo       566.10     54.00      512.10
                                        Sodium     1000.00   1959.00     -959.00
                                        Fiber        30.00      1.33       28.67
◆Pork, cured, cooked, bacon,    2.00    Fat-Sat      27.96      7.30       20.66
 Breads, Cracked-wheat, slic    3.00     - Mono      27.96     12.40       15.56
 Best Foods Real Mayonnaise     2.00     - Poly      27.96     12.30       15.66
 Tomatoes, raw, 2 3/5 in dia    1.00     -Total      83.87     34.00       49.87
 Lettuce, raw, Crisphead, as    1.00    Iron         10.00      6.20        3.80
                                        Calcium    1000.00    169.00      831.00



F1 Help        F3 Graph        F5 Add Food    F7 Copy for... F9 Preview
F2 Tables      F4 Day Planner  F6 Mk Standard F8 Show Nutr % F10 Done
```

Figure 10.2 Slim has already exceeded his daily dose of salt.

measurements can get a little fuzzy. To help, Health and Diet Pro contains a feature that lets you determine the food content of whatever you cook.

To analyze your recipe, type the name, food group, serving size, and number of servings of the recipe. You then combine items from the food list according to your recipe. Health and Diet Pro does the rest, determining the measurements for the entire recipe and for a single serving. You then can experiment with the recipe to make a healthier entree.

YOUR PERSONAL MEDICAL ADVISOR Some doctors don't tell you much. They diagnose your illness, give you a prescription to cure it, and send you on your way. You may never understand what was wrong with you or why the prescription helped. With Home Medical Advisor, you can get the information you need at the press of a key. The program offers a complete medical library containing the following volumes:

- *Symptom file*. If you get sick and you don't know what you have, go to the Symptom file. Select

TIP
Cut down on sodium and fats. Be creative when designing your recipes. For example, try to substitute an herb or spice for salt, or try using one of the commercial flavored salt substitutes.

your symptom from the list of symptoms to determine what is ailing you (see Figure 10.3).

- *Disease file*. If you know what you have or if you are curious about a disease, go to the Disease file. This file lists common diseases and provides information about each disease listed.

- *Injury file*. This file contains a list of common injuries, including insect and animal bites, cuts and bruises, head injuries, and broken bones.

- *Poison file*. The poison file is a good file to read *before* you need it. It lists various poisons by chemical and product name and explains emergency procedures in the event that such a product is ingested, poured on the skin, or splashed in the eyes.

- *Test file*. This file contains a list of commonly performed diagnostic tests. If your physician orders one of these tests for you, you can get more information about the test from this file.

- *Rx-Drug file*. Many pharmacies currently offer a system that provides information about the drugs you are taking. When you pick up your prescription, the pharmacist prints out a page or two telling you about the drug, about possible side effects, and about possible interactions with other drugs. If you don't have such a service, the Rx-Drug file can help you get this same information.

TIP
Be prepared. It is much easier to deal with an emergency if you are prepared for it, especially when the emergency deals with a poisonous substance. Get emergency information *before* you need it.

- *Referral file*. Initially, this file contains information describing the Referral file. If you send your warranty/registration card for Home Medical Advisor, the software company (Pixel Perfect) will send you a listing of the board-certified physicians, hospitals, and clinics in your area.

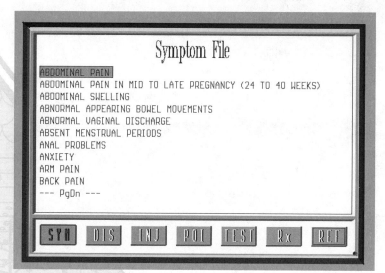

Figure 10.3 Choose your symptom.

In addition to providing useful medical information, Home Medical Advisor is easy to use. You simply select the item you want to look up from the items listed. The program displays the information, as shown in Figure 10.4.

The program also offers a *hypertext* system that links information about one item to related information about another item. To do this, the program displays the linked word or term in a different color or highlights it on the information screen. To jump to the screen that contains related information, you select the word using your mouse or the arrow keys. If you want to go back to a previous screen, just keep pressing Esc until you're there.

Figure 10.4 Select an item to get additional information.

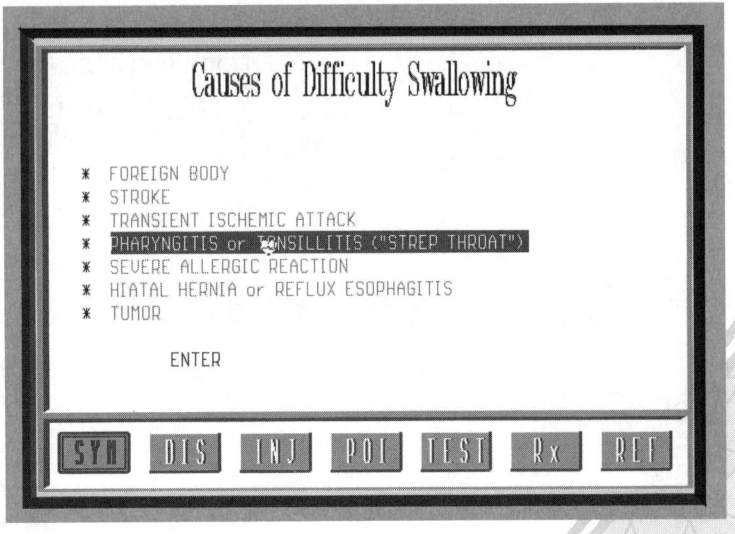

A FINAL WORD ABOUT HEALTH AND DIET PROGRAMS

Although you can get all the information you need about health and diet from books and magazines, Health and Diet Pro and Home Medical Advisor allow you to customize the information and apply it to your particular situation. These programs also put the information within the reach of your keyboard. Because the information is so easy to get, you can take more control of your own health.

Causes of Difficulty Swallowing

* FOREIGN BODY
* STROKE
* TRANSIENT ISCHEMIC ATTACK
* PHARYNGITIS or TONSILLITIS ("STREP THROAT")
* SEVERE ALLERGIC REACTION
* HIATAL HERNIA or REFLUX ESOPHAGITIS
* TUMOR

ENTER

SYM   DIS   INJ   POI   TEST   Rx   REF

11

GET COOKIN' WITH YOUR PC

Okay, I'll admit it, the chapter title is a little misleading. Your PC cannot beat eggs, sauté vegetables, or baste a chicken. What it can do, with the right software, is provide you with a collection of menus and a way to organize your own menus. It can then help you modify the menus by changing the serving size and ingredients, let you find recipes for the ingredients you have on hand, and print a shopping list for you. As you'll see in this chapter, you can do all this and more with Micro Cookbook.

MORE THAN JUST A RECIPE BOOK Micro Cookbook comes with 350 recipes for dishes that range from cucumber sandwiches to Norwegian meatballs, and you can purchase additional disks that contain many other recipes. As shown in Figure 11.1, the opening screen allows you to look up a recipe in a variety of ways: by recipe name, by ingredients, or by classification. To look up a recipe by name, for example, simply press F1 to display a list of recipes and then select the one you want. The program displays the ingredients on-screen. By pressing Enter, you can view the cooking instructions. You even can print a copy of the recipe on an index card or on a regular sheet of paper to take with you or share with a friend.

Figure 11.1 Looking up recipes is a snap.

Micro Cookbook is much more than just an ordinary cookbook that helps you find recipes, as you'll see in the following sections.

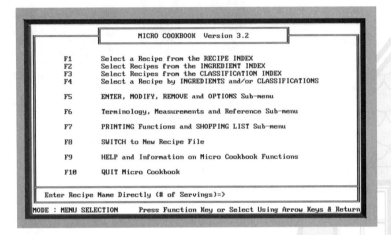

```
┌─────────────────────────────────────────────────────────────┐
│              ┌───────────────────────────────────┐           │
│              │    MICRO COOKBOOK  Version 3.2    │           │
│              └───────────────────────────────────┘           │
│                                                               │
│     F1        Select a Recipe from the RECIPE INDEX           │
│     F2        Select Recipes from the INGREDIENT INDEX        │
│     F3        Select Recipes from the CLASSIFICATION INDEX    │
│     F4        Select a Recipe by INGREDIENTS and/or CLASSIFICATIONS │
│                                                               │
│     F5        ENTER, MODIFY, REMOVE and OPTIONS Sub-menu      │
│                                                               │
│     F6        Terminology, Measurements and Reference Sub-menu│
│                                                               │
│     F7        PRINTING Functions and SHOPPING LIST Sub-menu   │
│                                                               │
│     F8        SWITCH to New Recipe File                       │
│                                                               │
│     F9        HELP and Information on Micro Cookbook Functions │
│                                                               │
│     F10       QUIT Micro Cookbook                             │
│                                                               │
│  ┌──────────────────────────────────────────────────────┐   │
│  │ Enter Recipe Name Directly (# of Servings)=>          │   │
│  └──────────────────────────────────────────────────────┘   │
│ MODE : MENU SELECTION    Press Function Key or Select Using Arrow Keys & Return │
└─────────────────────────────────────────────────────────────┘
```

DO YOU FEEL LIKE CHICKEN TONIGHT? Micro Cookbook offers various ways to look up recipes, one of which is a classification index. In the mood for Italian food? Press F3 to display the Classification index shown in Figure 11.2 and choose Italian; you get a list of 26 Italian dishes. Need a vegetable to go along with your steak? Choose Vegetable for a list of 32 vegetable dishes.

WHAT'S IN THE FRIDGE? You're hungry. You just got home from work and the last thing you want to do is go to the grocery store. You have a can of tomatoes, half an onion, and some leftover chicken. What can you make? To find out, press F4 to display the Ingredients and Classification

TIP
No more food-stained recipe cards. With Micro Cookbook, the recipe remains on your computer disk. If you ever lose the recipe or get it dirty, simply print a new copy.

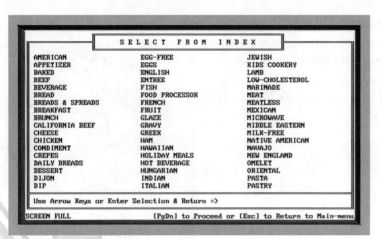

Figure 11.2 In the mood for a type of food?

index, shown in Figure 11.3. Type the ingredients you have, and the program will find a recipe that uses those ingredients.

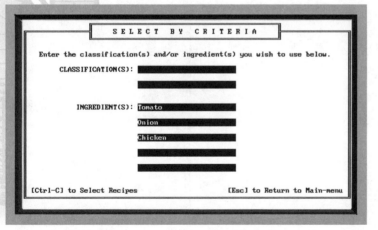

Figure 11.3 Find recipes for the ingredients you have on hand.

THE RECIPE SERVES FOUR BUT I'M HAVING SEVEN . . .

With typical cookbooks, the recipe specifies the number of servings and tells you how much of each ingredient to add. If you want to cook more or fewer servings, you have to calculate the amount of each ingredient. With Micro Cookbook, the program does it for you.

WHAT DO I NEED FROM THE GROCERY STORE? Once you've determined what you want to cook, simply enter the name of each recipe on the shopping list and type any additional items you need from the store. Micro Cookbook prints a detailed shopping list, like the one shown in Figure 11.4.

TIP
Check your list. Before you run out to the store with your new printout, check the list to find out if you already have some of the ingredients.

```
** SHOPPING LIST

BREAD CRUMBS          BROCCOLI            BUTTER
CHICKEN BREAST        CHIVES              EGG
FLOUR                 GARLIC              LEMON JUICE
OLIVE OIL             PARSLEY             PEPPER
POTATO                SALT                VEGETABLE OIL
WATER


    INGREDIENT           RECIPE                QTY    MEASURE     PREPARED
    ==========           ======                ===    =======
    BREAD CRUMBS         CHICKEN KIEV          2      cups

    BROCCOLI             LEMON BROCCOLI        1      bunch

    BUTTER               CHICKEN KIEV          1/2    Lb.

    CHICKEN BREAST       CHICKEN KIEV          4                  boned, ski..

    CHIVES               CHICKEN KIEV          2      Tbl.        chopped

    EGG                  CHICKEN KIEV          2                  beaten

    FLOUR                CHICKEN KIEV          2      cups        white

    GARLIC               LEMON BROCCOLI        1      clove       minced

    LEMON JUICE          LEMON BROCCOLI        2      Tbl.

    OLIVE OIL            LEMON BROCCOLI        1/4    cup

    PARSLEY              CHICKEN KIEV          2      Tbl.        chopped

    PEPPER               CHICKEN KIEV          3/4    tsp.        white
                         SHOESTRING POTATOES

    POTATO               SHOESTRING POTATOES   4      large       Idaho

    SALT                 CHICKEN KIEV          1/2    tsp.
                         SHOESTRING POTATOES
                         LEMON BROCCOLI        1      tsp.

    VEGETABLE OIL        CHICKEN KIEV
                         SHOESTRING POTATOES                      for deep-f..

    WATER                LEMON BROCCOLI        6      cup         boiling
```

Figure 11.4 Micro Cookbook can help with your shopping.

ADDING YOUR OWN RECIPES In addition to providing you with 350 recipes, Micro Cookbook lets you add your own recipes. Press F5 to display the Enter, Modify, Remove, and Options submenu, and then press F2 to add your recipe.

You can further customize Micro Cookbook by editing recipes that came with the program or by deleting recipes that you never use. This gives the program more room for handling the recipes you add.

ADDING OTHER COOKBOOKS TO YOUR LIBRARY If you like the recipes included in Micro Cookbook and you're hungry for more, you can purchase these additional cookbooks from Pinpoint Software for about twenty bucks each:

Appetizers	*Kid's Cookery*
Breads and Spreads	*Meatless Meals*
California Beef	*Microwave Cooking*
Daily Breads	*Recipe Express ($35)*
Desserts	*Soups and Salads*
Food Processor	*Special Diet Recipes*
Holiday Meals	*Wok Cooking*

12 DIGGING UP YOUR ROOTS

Most of us are interested in finding out where we came from. We know who our parents are and we usually know a little about our grandparents, but beyond that, things get a little fuzzy. Of course we had great-grandparents and great-great-grandparents, but where did they came from? What did they do for a living? And how and when did they die? All this information can be engrossing, if you just had some way to collect it and organize it. In this chapter, we look at a program that can help you dig up the roots of your family tree: Family Tree Maker.

IT'S AS SIMPLE AS FILLING IN THE BLANKS When you first start Family Tree Maker, the program asks you a series of questions about your computer system, including what kind of printer you have and how you want information displayed. It then displays an index card like the one shown in Figure 12.1. You type the requested information, pressing the Tab key to move from line to line.

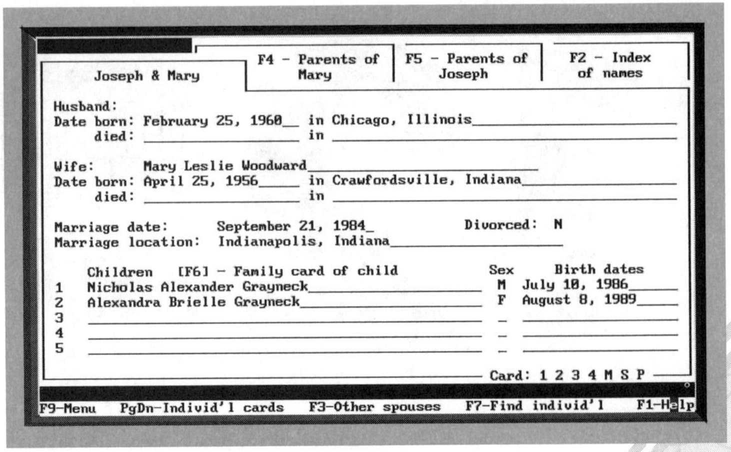

Figure 12.1 Supply the requested information.

This first card is a *family card*. It allows you to enter information about your spouse and about any children you have. If you are not married, type information only about yourself. When you finish filling out the family card, you can fill out four *individual cards* for any person in your family. These four cards, shown in Figure 12.2, allow you to enter the following information:

- *Birthdate and location.* It often is interesting to see how various generations migrate from state to state or country to country. It also is interesting to compare the date when a couple got married with the date on which their first child was born.

- *Special events.* Use these blanks to record any special awards or degrees a person has earned or any other accomplishments.

- *Relation to parents: Natural, Adopted, or Foster.* If a person is adopted or is a foster child, you can note that here.

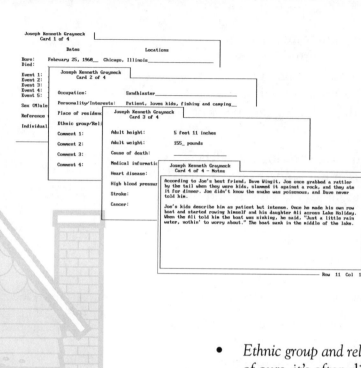

Figure 12.2 Enter additional information.

Joseph Kenneth Grayneck
Card 1 of 4

Dates   Locations

Born: February 25, 1968__ Chicago, Illinois_____
Died:

Event 1:   Joseph Kenneth Grayneck
Event 2:   Card 2 of 4
Event 3:
Event 4:   Occupation: Sandblaster_____
Event 5:
            Personality/Interests: Patient, loves kids, fishing and camping__
Sex (M)ale
            Place of residen   Joseph Kenneth Grayneck
Reference   Card 3 of 4
            Ethnic group/Rel
Individual
            Comment 1:   Adult height: 5 feet 11 inches
            Comment 2:   Adult weight: 155_ pounds
            Comment 3:   Cause of death:
            Comment 4:   Medical informatic   Joseph Kenneth Grayneck
                          Heart disease: Card 4 of 4 - Notes
                          High blood pressur According to Joe's best friend, Dave Wingit, Joe once grabbed a rattler
                                              by the tail when they were kids, slammed it against a rock, and they ate
                          Stroke: it for dinner. Joe didn't know the snake was poisonous, and Dave never
                                              told him.
                          Cancer:
                                              Joe's kids describe him as patient but intense. Once he made his own row
                                              boat and started rowing himself and his daughter Ali across Lake Holiday.
                                              When the Ali told him the boat was sinking, he said, "Just a little rain
                                              water, nothin' to worry about." The boat sank in the middle of the lake.

                                                                    ─ Row 11 Col 1

- *Occupation, personality, and interests.* The Occupation section is especially interesting, in that it lets you trace your family's progress from generation to generation or view occupational trends.

- *Ethnic group and religion.* In this great melting pot of ours, it's often difficult for us to trace our ethnic and religious heritage. The entries here can clarify just how mixed up your gene pool really is.

- *Height, weight, and medical history.* By entering facts about each person's medical history, you can trace possible hereditary illnesses. You can now find out which side of the family is responsible for your kid's chronic earaches.

- *Notes.* You can add up to five pages of notes containing anything at all: short stories, a person's favorite joke or saying, or a description of the person.

TIP
Missing information?
Don't worry if you are missing some information. You can send the unfinished tree to your relatives and ask them to supply any information they may have.

PRINTING YOUR FAMILY TREE As you enter information, you may not think Family Tree Maker is all that impressive. It's during the printing operation that the program demonstrates its expertise. It takes the information you entered and allows you to print the following four types of family trees:

- *Ancestor*. This is a family tree showing the selected person and any of his or her predecessors. You can choose to go back as far as the information you entered allows you (see Figure 12.3).

- *Descendant*. This is a family tree showing the selected person, any of his or her offspring, and any of their offspring. Again, you can go as far down the family tree as your information allows.

- *Photo*. This option is a short family tree showing a person with his or her parents. The box for each person is enlarged to allow you to paste a photograph inside the box.

- *Direct descendant*. This is an abbreviated family tree that shows a direct line of descent between two people. For example, you might choose a woman and her great-great grandfather. The program then displays only those people that are in the line of descent between the man and his great-great granddaughter.

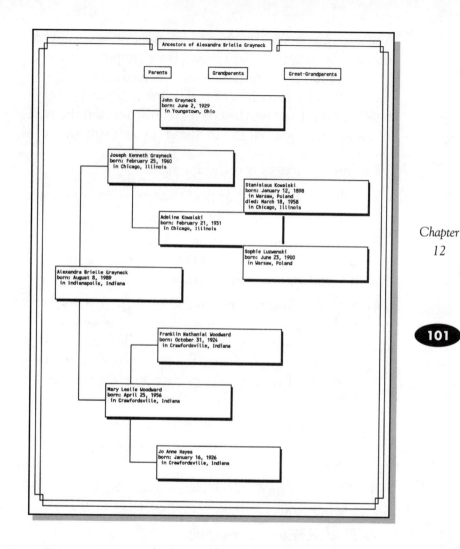

Figure 12.3 Use the ancestor tree to track your roots.

You also can choose the types of information you want to include for each individual listed. For example, you can have the program print the name, age, birthdate, and medical history of each person. The following steps show how easy it is to select the type of family tree and the type of information you want to include on your printout:

1. Press F9 to display the Main menu.

2. Select Print tree, and select the type of tree you want to print.

3. Select the person for whom you want to print the tree. That is, choose the person whose ancestors or descendents you want to show.

4. Select to print the tree on a single page or across multiple pages. A screen appears offering several options; you can choose to print a title and/or footnote on the page, change the border style or the style of boxes, change the information in each box (see Figure 12.4), or change other print settings.

5. If you want to change any of the options listed, press the designated key and follow the on-screen instructions.

6. When you are finished selecting options, press F10 to see how your family tree will look in print.

7. To start printing, press Enter.

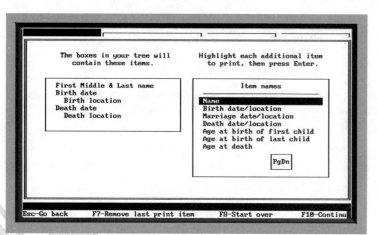

The boxes in your tree will contain these items.

Highlight each additional item to print, then press Enter.

First Middle & Last name
Birth date
　Birth location
Death date
　Death location

Item names
━━━━━━━━━━━
Name
Birth date/location
Marriage date/location
Death date/location
Age at birth of first child
Age at birth of last child
Age at death

| PgDn |

Esc-Go back   F7-Remove last print item   F8-Start over   F10-Continue

Figure 12.4 Print selected information for each person.

WHO IS SHE TO US? Every family gets into discussions about various relatives and their relationships to other members of the family. "Is Mary a second cousin or a first cousin once removed?" And what actually makes a person a bona fide aunt or uncle? With Family Tree Maker, you have instant answers to such questions:

1. Press F9 to display the Main menu.

2. Select Options and then Kinship. Family Tree Maker displays a list of everyone in your family tree.

3. Select the two relatives you want to know about. The program displays their relationship, as shown in Figure 12.5.

CREATING A BIRTHDAY AND ANNIVERSARY CALENDAR Now that you have all your relatives' birthdays and anniversaries entered in one file, wouldn't it be nice if you could pull that information into a birthday calendar? With Family Tree Maker you can print such a calendar.

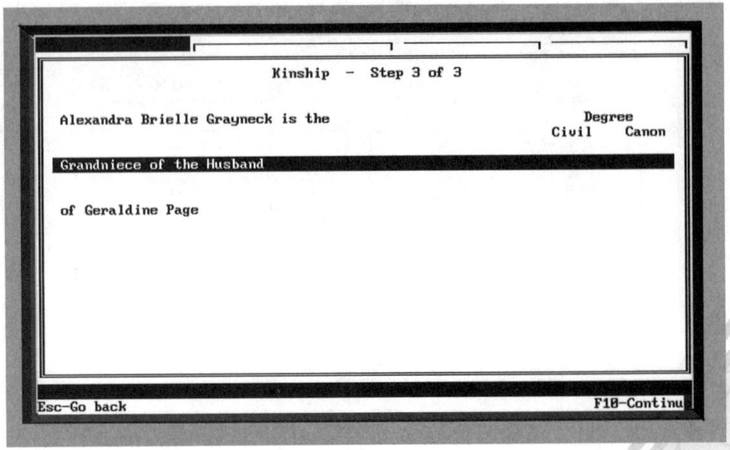

Figure 12.5 Find out if Aunt Mildred is really your aunt.

OTHER FAMILY TREE MAKERS? NAH! With a suggested retail price of sixty bucks and a street price of around forty bucks, you can't do much better than Family Tree Maker. Besides the fact that the program is easy to use, has plenty of useful features, and produces great printouts, it comes complete with some of the best documentation I've ever seen. The book provides clear instructions, plenty of art and examples, and includes a bibliography, a thorough index, and suggestions and resources for helping you search for information about your long lost relatives. It even comes with several sheets of high-quality paper to give your family tree a professional touch.

Kinship – Step 3 of 3

Alexandra Brielle Grayneck is the

Degree
Civil   Canon

Grandniece of the Husband

of Geraldine Page

Esc–Go back   F18–Continu

13

BECOMING YOUR OWN CUSTOM PUBLISHER

Desktop publishing is one of the most exciting and rewarding of computer activities. Out of nothing, you create pages that express your own ideas and sense of style. It is the ultimate challenge—to transform a blank page into something that is informative, useful, and beautiful. In this chapter, we look at a few programs that give you control of the page: The New Print Shop, BannerMania, and Express Publisher.

CREATING CARDS AND ANNOUNCEMENTS FOR ALL OCCASIONS

Remember those carefree Crayola days, when you used to *make* cards for your mom and dad? You would put your own special messages inside and draw and color your own pictures. Cards meant something back then. Nowadays, it seems that only professional greeting-card authors and artists have the right to think up clever ideas for cards. And you have to pay steep prices for their mass market creations.

With The New Print Shop, you can travel back to those earlier days and put together a professional-looking card that expresses your own personal touch. You work through a series of screens, as shown in Figure 13.1, to select just how you want the card laid out, what kind of border you want to use, what kind of picture you want to put on the front, and what you want the inside of the card to look like. You even get to compose your own personal messages.

Figure 13.1 Use The New Print Shop to create greeting cards.

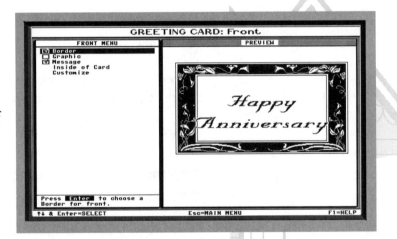

Although the greeting-card feature is probably the most popular feature of The New Print Shop, the program lets you create many more custom publications, including:

- *Invitations and announcements.*
  Create your own invitations for showers, anniversaries, and parties, or create announcements for births and graduations.

- *Stationery and letterheads.* Create your own letterhead complete with a picture at the top and your address and phone number at the bottom, as shown in Figure 13.2.

- *Banners.* Create *Happy Birthday!* or *Welcome Home!* or *It's a Girl!* banners. Print Shop will print on several pages, allowing you to make large banners to impress your friends and neighbors.

- *Signs.* Need a sign or flyers for a garage sale or open house? Print Shop is there to help. You can enter the date, time, and location of the event, include a phone number where you can be reached, or even use the graphics editor to draw a map to your house.

- *Calendars.* You select the month you want to print, and Print Shop takes care of the rest. You can type dates to remember or mark special dates with a picture.

- *Wrapping paper.* Cover a sheet of paper with pictures or clever sayings and then wrap a gift with it. Your gift will stand out in the stack.

HAVING FUN WITH BANNERS AND SIGNS If you really like to play with banners and signs, and you've exhausted the banner feature of The New Print Shop, consider getting BannerMania. BannerMania takes the banner feature of Print Shop and breathes new life into it, making your text and graphics do cartwheels.

As with The New Print Shop, BannerMania leads you through the process of creating a banner. You select how

TIP
Adding color. If you have a printer that can print different colors, you can use Print Shop to create colorful cards. If not, you can add your own color with crayons or markers, or print on colored paper.

Caffeine & Cakes
Joe and Mary Dunlap, Proprietors

1311 East Pike
Crawfordsville, IN 43098
(317) 894-8375

Figure 13.2 Create your own stationery and letterhead.

Figure 13.3 Let BannerMania transmogrify your banner.

you want the banner laid out, and you enter the text you want to include on the banner. The program does the rest. When you are finished, you can enter a command to *transmogrify* the banner. BannerMania then puts on a show for you, creating various incarnations of your banner. A snapshot of a banner being transmogrified is shown in Figure 13.3. When you see something you like, simply press Esc twice to select it.

109

PRINTING YOUR OWN NEWSLETTERS Newsletters are a great way to communicate your ideas, experiences, and other information to a number of people. If you have a large family and many friends, a newsletter may be the only practical way to keep them all informed. If you are part of a club or other organization, you can use a newsletter to keep all the members informed of upcoming dates and events. Or, if you run a business out of your home, a newsletter can help you drum up new business or keep current customers informed of new products and services.

Figure 13.4 Create your own newsletters.

Whatever the purpose, there are several inexpensive programs on the market that can help you publish your own newsletter. One of these programs, called Express Publisher, even contains a newsletter template. The first page of the newsletter is already laid out, as shown in Figure 13.4. All you have to do is insert text and pictures into the boxes (called *frames*).

To place text in a frame, you can type the text directly into the frame or *import* the text from a file you created in your word processing program. For example, if you type a story using Word 5.0 and save it in a file, you can import the story into a frame.

You can import pictures as well. Express Publisher comes with several graphic images. After importing a picture, you can use your mouse to drag the image anywhere on the page or to change its size and dimensions. You can even plop the picture down on top of some text and have the program wrap the text around the object, as shown in the figure.

TIP

Insert real pictures. If you do a lot of publishing, consider purchasing a *scanner*, which allows you to bring photographs, logos, or any other art from paper into your computer.

Figure 13.5 Create your own customized business card.

GETTING DOWN TO BUSINESS

If you run a business out of your home, you can use a desktop publishing program to create a variety of customized publications for drumming up business and keeping in touch with your customers. You can create flyers for special sales, design and print your own advertisements and coupons for newspapers and magazines, and even create your own business cards, as shown in Figure 13.5.

OTHER DESKTOP PUBLISHING PROGRAMS

There is a wide range of desktop publishing programs on the market. If you are looking for something to use around the house for small (one to two pages) publications, look at Express Publisher, Publish It! or—if you have Microsoft Windows—Microsoft Publisher. If you want to create larger publications, look at Aldus PageMaker, Ventura Publisher, and Framemaker.

Chapter 13

111

TIP
Publishing with a word processor? Many word processing programs, including WordPerfect 5.1 and Word for Windows 2.0, contain desktop publishing features.

14 DYING AND PAYING TAXES

The Berlin wall comes crashing down, the USSR loses the cold war, and Johnny Carson retires. Nothing is certain anymore. Nothing except the inevitability of death and taxes. In this chapter, we look at two programs that can help you deal with these depressing activities: WillMaker and Turbo Tax.

DRAWING UP YOUR OWN WILL In addition to the fact that they are both depressing ideas, wills and taxes have something else in common: in both cases, we try to keep other people from determining what happens to our money and possessions. In the case of a will, we try to make sure that when we die, our stuff and our children go to the right people. With WillMaker and about an hour of free time, you can create your own *simple will* to do the following:

- *Name beneficiaries.* You can make up to 28 separate gifts to your spouse, your children, your friends, charity organizations, or any other individual or group.

- *Name alternate beneficiaries.* If a beneficiary dies fewer than 45 days after you die, that person doesn't get the gift you left him. (Of course, that person doesn't need the gift you left.) In such a case, the gift goes to the alternate beneficiary.

- *Designate a person to take all the stuff that's left.* After accounting for the gifts, a large chunk of your estate may be left. You can name a person, several people, or an organization to receive whatever's left.

- *Name a guardian for your children.* If you have children, you can name a person or couple to care for your children in the event that both you and your spouse die.

- *Name someone to manage your children's property.* If you leave money and property to a child under the age of 18, it's probably a good idea to have a person or an institution make sure the money gets spent right—a teenager can blow a lot of money on prom night.

- *Name an executor.* Every will must name an executor or representative who is in charge of making sure the directives in the will are carried out.

- *Cancel debts owed to you.* If someone owes you money, you may want to let them off the hook when you die.

INFORMATION
Simple will versus living will. WillMaker lets you create a simple will for distributing property. A living will tells your doctor and hospital whether or not to administer life-support systems in the event you are incapacitated.

- *Specify how you want debts and expenses paid.* If you owe money upon your death, you can specify where you want the money taken from to pay your debts, expenses, and taxes.

How difficult is it to make a will? If you need to create a straightforward will (for example, you want to leave everything to your spouse and children and name a guardian for your children), the process is easy. WillMaker asks you a series of questions, as shown in Figure 14.1. For more complex situations, you may need to consult the book that comes with WillMaker or hire a lawyer.

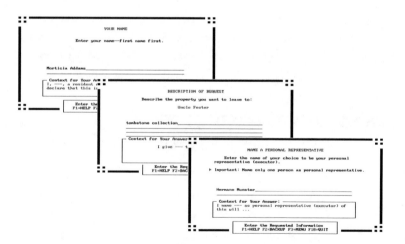

Figure 14.1 With WillMaker, you answer a series of questions.

When you finish answering the questions, WillMaker lets you display your will on-screen, print your will, save the will as a text file, or go back and change the will.

MAKING TAXES LESS TAXING The Internal Revenue Service is currently considering a plan to revamp the Federal tax program. With the new plan, the correct amount of money would be deducted from each person's paycheck; you would no longer have to file a tax return. In Britain, in Germany, and in several other developed countries, such a system is already in place. Until we have such a system, however, we have to deal with the annual tax return.

To help us get through this difficult time, several software companies have created specialized tax programs. In Turbo Tax, for example, you enter your tax information, and the program determines which forms you need to fill out and how much money the IRS owes you or how much money you owe.

AN INTERVIEW WITH A TAX EXPERT With Turbo Tax, you can complete your tax return in any of the following three ways:

- *Interview.* Turbo Tax asks you a series of questions, that lead you through the process of filling out the proper forms.

- *Tax Forms.* This option displays a personal information sheet on which you enter your name, address, social security number, and other general information. When you are finished, you can

TIP
Other ways to leave money. The book that comes with WillMaker points out that there may be better ways to leave money than by using a will.

select the forms and schedules you need to fill out.

- *File Cabinet*. The File Cabinet provides a list of deductions and other items you may want to include in your tax return, such as child care and business expenses. You choose the item, and Turbo Tax displays the form you need to fill out.

FORMS, FORMS, AND MORE FORMS One of the most difficult parts of completing your tax return is figuring out which forms you have to fill out and then getting them. You may drive to the library, the post office, the bank, and several other institutions to find the forms you need. With Turbo Tax, all the forms are conveniently stored on your disk. Turbo Tax even helps you figure out which forms you need, as shown in Figure 14.2.

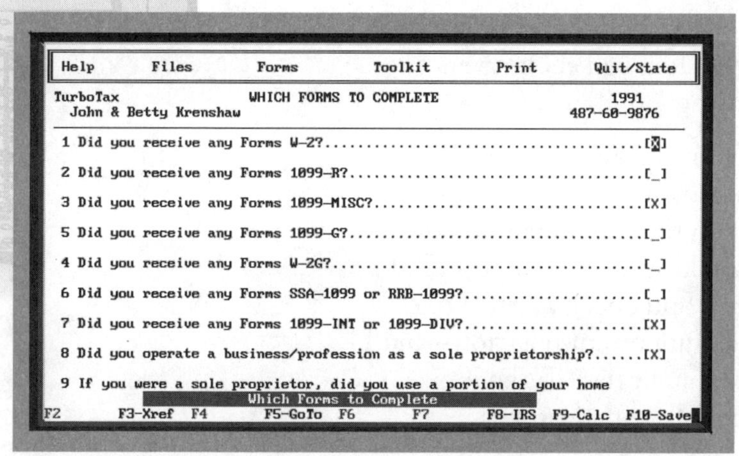

Figure 14.2 Turbo Tax helps you determine the forms you need.

PLAYING WHAT IF? Most tax programs allow you to play *What If* with your tax return. What if I choose not to itemize; would I save money? What if I choose to deduct my points over the life of the loan; how much will that cost me this year? With Turbo Tax, you enter the What If command and then play with the figures, as shown in Figure 14.3.

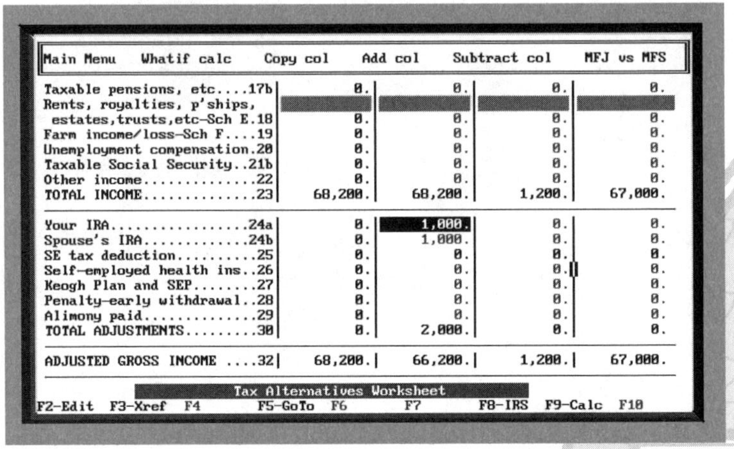

Figure 14.3 Play What If to determine your best tax strategy.

```
Main Menu   Whatif calc   Copy col   Add col   Subtract col   MFJ vs MFS

Taxable pensions, etc....17b        0.          0.           0.            0.
Rents, royalties, p'ships,
  estates,trusts,etc-Sch E.18       0.          0.           0.            0.
Farm income/loss-Sch F....19        0.          0.           0.            0.
Unemployment compensation.20        0.          0.           0.            0.
Taxable Social Security..21b        0.          0.           0.            0.
Other income.............22         0.          0.           0.            0.
TOTAL INCOME.............23     68,200.     68,200.      1,200.       67,000.

Your IRA.................24a         0.      1,000.           0.            0.
Spouse's IRA.............24b         0.      1,000.           0.            0.
SE tax deduction.........25          0.          0.           0.            0.
Self-employed health ins..26         0.          0.          0.            0.
Keogh Plan and SEP.......27          0.          0.           0.            0.
Penalty-early withdrawal.28          0.          0.           0.            0.
Alimony paid.............29          0.          0.           0.            0.
TOTAL ADJUSTMENTS........30          0.      2,000.           0.            0.

ADJUSTED GROSS INCOME ....32|    68,200.|    66,200.|     1,200.|      67,000.
                         Tax Alternatives Worksheet
F2-Edit  F3-Xref  F4      F5-GoTo  F6       F7        F8-IRS  F9-Calc  F10
```

FREE CONSULTATIONS As you are filling out your federal tax return, you have to answer some questions. For example, if you bought a house this year, you may be wondering whether or not you can deduct the points you paid. If you run a business out of your home, you may need to know whether you can claim your home as a business deduction. With Turbo Tax, you get answers to these questions simply by pressing Alt-F1.

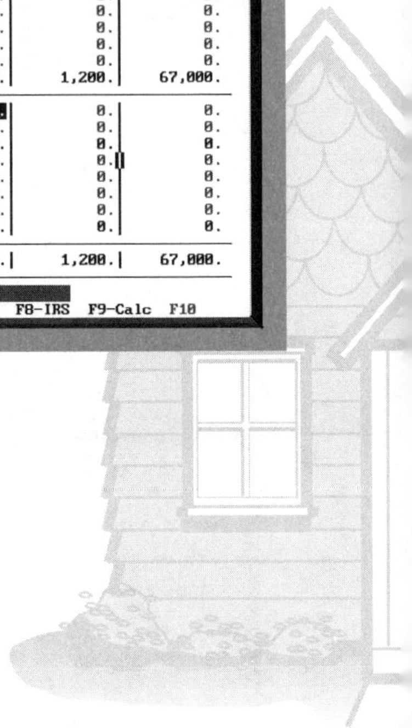

A PRELIMINARY AUDIT I don't know about you, but I get pretty nervous just as I'm inserting my tax return into the envelope. All sorts of doubts run through my mind. Did I remember to enter the kids' social security numbers? Did I fill out all the appropriate forms and check all the boxes I needed to check? And the most important question—did I do anything that might raise an audit flag? Turbo Tax can put your mind at ease with the following features:

- *Data Examiner.* Checks your return for missing or contradictory information and displays a list of any problems it finds. Problems you must correct are marked with an asterisk (*).

- *List of overrides and notes.* If you choose to override a calculated field (an entry that Turbo Tax calculated automatically), this feature displays the override to make sure you still want to override that information.

- *Tax saving suggestions.* This feature looks at your return and determines whether there are any areas where you could save money. For example, if you took a standard deduction, the program suggests that you may be able to save money by itemizing.

- *IRS audit flags.* The program analyzes your tax return in much the same way an IRS employee would look at your return. The program then displays any areas that might cause the IRS to look at your return more closely.

- *U.S. averages.* If you itemize your deductions, you can have Turbo Tax compare your deductions against the national average to determine if they exceed the average.

You can have Turbo Tax perform any one of these checks or all the checks at once. If Turbo Tax finds a problem, it displays a window such as the one in Figure 14.4.

Figure 14.4 Turbo Tax performs an audit.

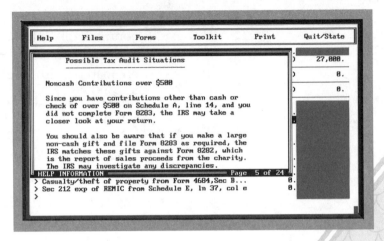

OTHER TAX AND LEGAL PROGRAMS Although WillMaker and Turbo Tax are leaders in the will-making and tax program fields, there are other fine programs on the market. If you need a general law program, check out the following two:

- *Home Lawyer (Hyatt Legal Services)*. Lets you create simple and living wills, powers of attorney, employment agreements, offer-of-employment letters, loan agreements, demands for money owed, bad check notices, credit report requests and corrections, leases, bills of sale, and defective-product complaint letters.

- *It's Legal*. Lets you create simple and living wills, powers of attorney, temporary guardianship agreements, loan agreements, and leases.

Likewise, tax programs abound. Some of the more popular are:

- *Andrew Tobias' Tax Cut*
- *EasyTax*

- *J.K. Lasser's Your Income Tax Software*
- *RapidTax*

15

CHECKBOOK BALANCING AND OTHER FINANCIAL TRICKS

How would you like to have your own personal accountant on your desk? Sound exciting? Well, it can be, assuming you have something exciting to do while your computer takes care of your finances. In this chapter, we look at two home finance programs that can manage your finances for you: Quicken 5.0 and WealthStarter.

WRITING CHECKS AND RECORDING TRANSACTIONS The problem with writing checks is that you have to enter a lot of duplicate information. You write the date on the check, the name of the person or business the check is for, the amount of the check (both numerically and spelled out), and a memo telling what the check is for. Then, you flip to your check register and enter all the same information again. If you happen to make a mistake copying the amount from your check to your register, you'll have lots of fun balancing your checkbook at the end of the month.

With Quicken, the date is entered automatically from your computer. You enter the name of the person or business the check is for, the check amount (only once), and a memo telling what the check is for. Quicken spells out the check amount on the check and enters the following information in the check register (see Figure 15.1):

- Today's date
- The check number
- Any address or memo you typed on the check
- The amount of the check
- The current balance

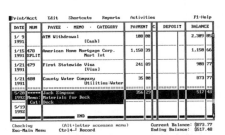

Figure 15.1 Quicken records the transaction.

This eliminates any discrepancies between what is written on the check and what appears in the register. It also eliminates any errors caused by miscalculations.

BALANCING YOUR CHECKBOOK There are three types of people in the world: those who can't balance their checkbook, those who hate doing it, and those who can't balance it and hate doing it. Face it—it's drudge work, and it's frustrating. You check and recheck, total and retotal until your eyes cross.

With Quicken, you simply mark the checks that have cleared, mark the deposits that are recorded on the bank statement, and enter any service charges. Quicken takes care of the rest, determining the total according to the register. If the total on your register does not match the total on the bank statement, Quicken lets you know, as shown in Figure 15.2. You still have to go back and compare the amounts of each check one by one. However, if you have to correct an amount, Quicken automatically recalculates the total in the register, saving you the time of recalculating the balance.

CREATING MONTHLY BUDGETS It's easy to see where your money comes from. You have one, maybe two, sources of income. Where your money goes is another matter. You have to pay gas, electric, and water bills; you may have bills for your children's education; you have car payments and repair bills, grocery bills, health and dental bills, credit card bills, and so on.

Figure 15.2 Quicken helps you balance your checkbook.

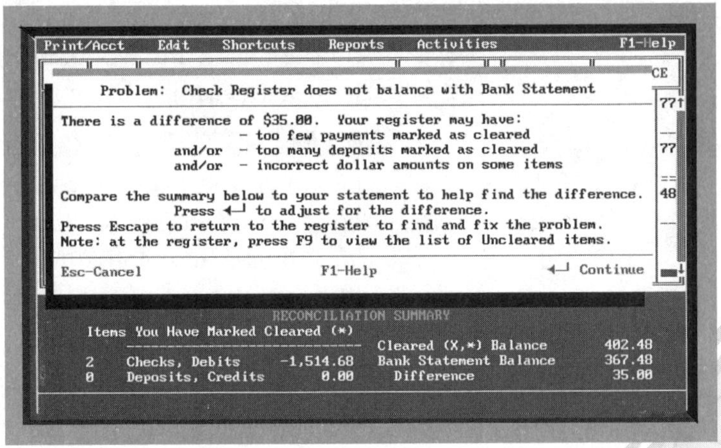

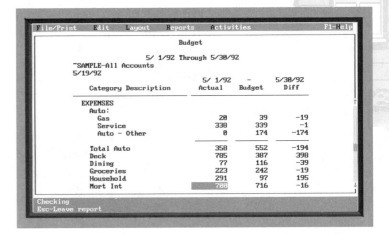

You know you should be tracking all these costs, but the mere thought of recording and totaling each expense makes your head spin. With Quicken, you can have the program keep track of each expense for you. Whenever you write a check, you specify the category of the expense. At the end of the month, you tell Quicken to generate a budget. Quicken takes care of the rest, as shown in Figure 15.3.

Figure 15.3 You always know where your money is going.

HOW MUCH WILL IT REALLY COST? AMORTIZING A LOAN

I hate borrowing money. And the reason I hate borrowing money is that I never know how much something is going to cost me. I go to buy a house for $60,000 and I end up paying $180,000. I buy a car for $10,000 and it costs me $12,000. I have a little hand-held calculator, and I'm pretty good at math, but I can never get my figures to match those of the real estate agent or of the salesperson at the car dealership. It must be that new math.

Because of this, I became very interested (my wife says obsessed) with amortization programs. Such programs perform the financial mumbo jumbo in the background and spit out numbers that reflect reality. You then can play with the numbers in private—without having some blood-sucking real estate agent telling you how much you can afford to pay for a house and how you can reduce your payments to free up some cash.

With Quicken's Loan Calculator, you simply enter the principal of the loan (how much money you want to borrow), the annual interest rate, and the term, and Quicken figures out the payment, as shown in Figure 15.4. Multiply the payment by the number of months you have to pay, and you know exactly how much the loan is going to cost you.

If you have a spreadsheet program (such as Excel, Lotus, or Quattro Pro), you can create your own loan calculator by using functions. Such a table is shown in Figure 15.5. You then can play What If with the numbers. What if the interest rate falls by .25%? How much will I save if I take out a 15-year mortgage instead of a 30-year mortgage? How will that affect my payments?

Figure 15.4 Quicken takes the guess-work out of loans.

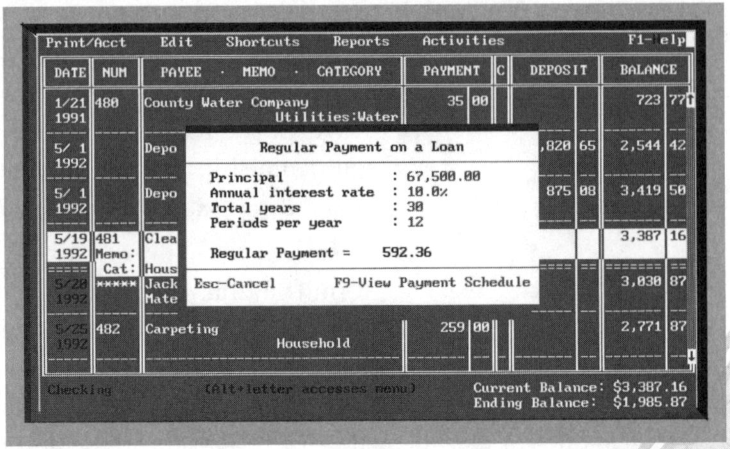

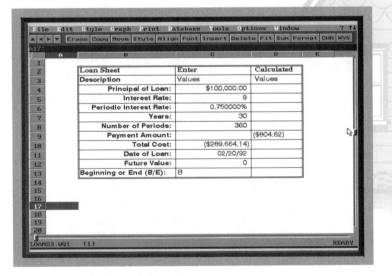

Figure 15.5 You can create your own loan calculator.

DON'T FORGET TO PAY YOUR BILLS! Quicken 5.0 offers a

feature called BillMinder, which helps you remember when to pay your bills. If a bill is due, a message appears on-screen, reminding you that you have some checks to write. You then can start Quicken and pay your bills immediately.

PAYING BILLS ELECTRONICALLY If your computer has a modem and is connected to the phone line, you can subscribe to an electronic bill-paying service. Instead of printing checks and then mailing them, you can pay them by phone, saving you the cost of postage and the time it takes to mail the bills. One such service, called CheckFree, pays up to 20 bills a month for $10. That's about twice the cost of postage, but depending on how much you have to pay for checks, the service can be cost-effective in addition to being convenient.

ACHIEVING YOUR FINANCIAL GOALS Once you have a handle on where all your money is going, you may want to start planning your future. You could invite a financial planner over to your house, but these folks never leave and you can't really trust them—they have a commission to make. Instead, consider getting WealthStarter, a financial planner that can help you set your own financial goals. You tell WealthStarter how much money is coming in, how much is going out, and then set your financial goals and specify a time frame, as shown in Figure 15.6. WealthStarter shows you how much money you have to save or invest each month to meet your goals.

WealthStarter comes complete with a fancy loan calculator (better than Quicken's), over 300 money management strategies from a proven expert (Charles Givens), and helpful tutorials on 16 financial subjects, including the following:

Figure 15.6 WealthStarter helps you realize your financial goals.

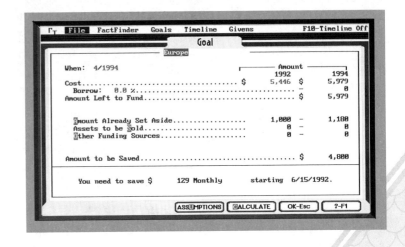

Mutual Funds

Planning Your Retirement

Buying a Home

Managing Your Debt

Understanding Insurance

Reducing Taxes

Saving for Your Children's Education

MOVING ON TO HIGH FINANCE If you are interested in investing money, you can move on to other financial programs to help you manage your investments. Although Quicken 5.0 and WealthStarter offer features that can help you keep track of your investments, you may want something that provides a little more information and guidance. If that's the case, consider WealthBuilder, an investment program created by the same company that makes WealthStarter.

16

NAVIGATING THE
HIGHWAY SYSTEM
WITH YOUR PC

Imagine this: You and your family are planning a trip from Chicago to Tampa, Florida. Your spouse has always wanted to go to the Grand Ole Opry, and you want to stop in Atlanta to visit your Uncle George and Aunt Louise. You sit down at your computer and type in your departure point and destination and the cities you want to visit along the way. In a few seconds, the computer shows you the best route to take to each city. But you decide you want to stay off the interstates. You tell the computer, and it reroutes you, using state highways and other roads. Well, you can stop imagining; with AutoMap, you can do all this and more.

GOING FROM POINT A TO POINT B With AutoMap, planning a trip can be as simple as entering your departure point and destination. You can do this in either of two ways. The most logical way (if you have a mouse) is to use the Route pull-down menu along with the map (see Figure 16.1). You select a starting point and a destination, and then specify the types of routes that you want calculated: Quickest, Shortest, Preferred, and Alternatives.

Figure 16.1 Specify a departure point and a destination.

AutoMap calculates one or more routes, displays a list of routes, and highlights the quickest route on the map, as shown in Figure 16.2. To take a detour to a city along the way, choose Add a via from the Route menu, and then specify the city you want to visit.

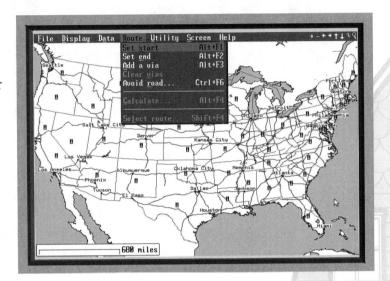

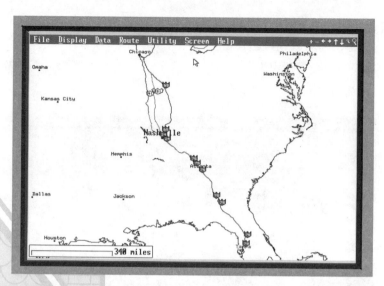

Figure 16.2 AutoMap finds the quickest route to take.

If you don't have a mouse, or if you would prefer typing the names of the departure and destination cities, you can display the Journey screen, shown in Figure 16.3. Type the name of the departure city, the time of departure, your destination, and any cities you want to visit along the way. The program even displays the distance you'll travel over the various routes.

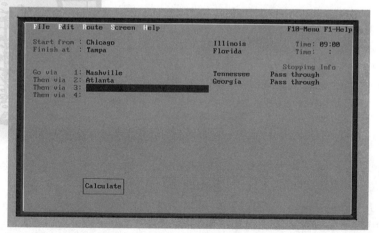

Figure 16.3 Tell AutoMap where you want to stop along the way.

STOPPING FOR DIRECTIONS

You've seen two of the main screens that make up AutoMap: the map itself and the Journey screen. There is one more screen to round out the trio: the Table screen, shown in

Figure 16.4. The Table translates the map into step-by-step directions telling you how far to travel on each leg of your journey, the name of each road you must take, and the exits to watch for.

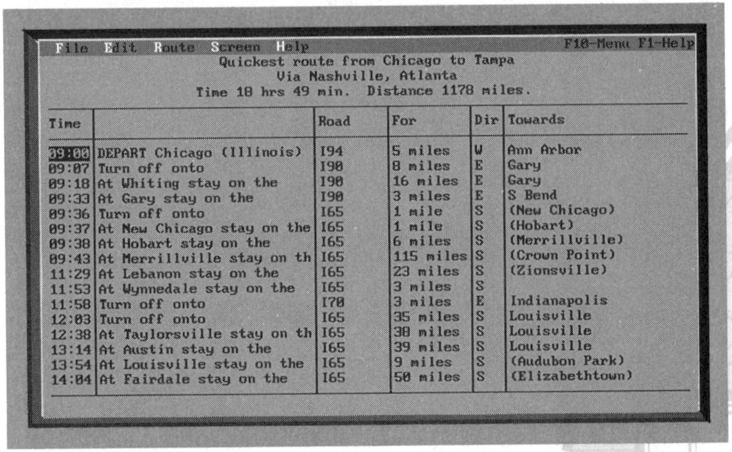

Figure 16.4 Get clear, step-by-step directions.

134

TAKING THE ROAD LESS TRAVELED
Some people are always in a hurry to get where they're going. They want to hop on the nearest interstate and be sucked to their destination by a roaring semi. Others prefer a more leisurely mode of travel. They want to travel the backroads, take in some scenery, and get a taste of the local cooking. No matter what your preference, AutoMap delivers. You simply enter your preferences, as shown in Figure 16.5, and AutoMap determines the best route for you. Don't like interstates? AutoMap will direct you around them. Like to ride the ferry? AutoMap will try to find some rivers without bridges.

SLOW DOWN, LEAD FOOT
In addition to being able to set your routing preferences, you can also specify how fast you like to drive (see Figure 16.6). By setting realistic speeds, you get a more accurate estimate of how long it will take you to get where you're going.

TIP
Quick switch from Map to Journey to Table.
AutoMap makes it easy to switch from one main screen to another. Press Alt-M for Map, Alt-J for Journey, or Alt-T for Table.

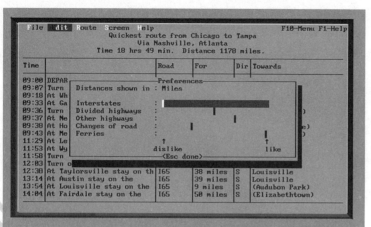

Figure 16.5 Specify your travel preferences.

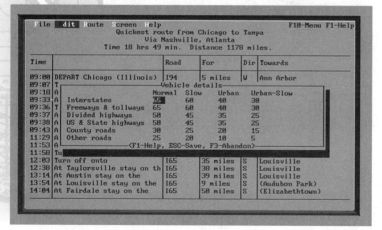

Figure 16.6 Set your own pace.

SEEING THE COUNTRYSIDE

Maybe you'd like to stop and fish along the way. Or maybe you want to visit a national park. You can have AutoMap include various details of the countryside, including lakes, mountain ranges, forests, parks, and even the Great Continental Divide.

PRINTING MAPS AND DIRECTIONS Once you've determined where you want to go and how you want to get there, you can print the map and directions. (Be sure to fold the paper several times to give your map the look and feel of a bona fide map.)

DO I HAVE TO WEAR A SEATBELT IN MAINE?
For every state on the map, AutoMap can display an information screen like the one shown in Figure 16.7, providing you with general information about the state, its driving laws, and phone numbers you can call for tourist information and road conditions.

Chapter 16

TIP
Avoid Construction. If you know of a section of a road that is under construction or that you want to avoid for some other reason, you can tell AutoMap to avoid that section.

Figure 16.7 Know something about the state you're visiting.

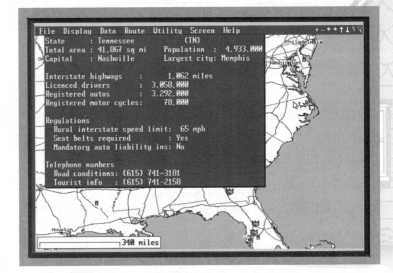

```
 File  Display  Data  Route  Utility  Screen  Help          + - + + ↑ ↓ ? ⟨
 State       : Tennessee          (TN)
 Total area  : 41,867 sq mi     Population   :  4,933,000
 Capital     : Nashville        Largest city: Memphis

 Interstate highways     :      1,062 miles
 Licenced drivers        :  3,058,000
 Registered autos        :  3,292,000
 Registered motor cycles :     78,000

 Regulations
   Rural interstate speed limit:  65 mph
   Seat belts required         :  Yes
   Mandatory auto liability ins:  No

 Telephone numbers
   Road conditions: (615) 741-3101
   Tourist info   : (615) 741-2158


            [      340 miles       ]
```

YOUR OWN AUTO TRAVEL AGENCY
Although AutoMap is good at giving directions, it doesn't quite stack up to a trip-planning kit from an automobile club. You can't find out about hotels or planned road construction. However, you can help your friends and family cut miles off their trips or plan a more scenic journey. Once everyone finds out that you have AutoMap, you might end up becoming the next Bargain Auto Travel Agency.

17

WIRING YOUR COMPUTER FOR SOUND

Most IBM and compatible computers are Neanderthal when it comes to producing sounds. Sure, they can beep to tell you when they're ready and when you've messed up, but your microwave oven can do that. If you want your computer to communicate using more sophisticated sounds, you have to add a sound board to your system, to the tune of $100 to $200. In this chapter, we look at the best sound board on the market— SoundBlaster Pro, and some of the neat software that comes with it.

WHY WIRE FOR SOUND? Most people purchase a sound board because they have a game program that can produce neat sounds. For example, you may have an aircraft fighter program that lets you hear the roar of the engines, missiles firing and blowing up, and maybe even your commander's voice. Without a sound board, these fancy sounds are buried in the program. A sound board can bring the sounds to life.

Other people who are interested in sound boards are musicians. The sound board gives the musician the ability to play music on the computer using a standard computer keyboard or a specially designed piano keyboard. With the proper software, a musician can write music on the computer, have the computer play the music back, and then go back and edit the music as needed.

But you don't need games and you don't have to be a musician to have fun with SoundBlaster Pro. SoundBlaster Pro comes with several programs that let you experiment with sound.

BEFORE YOU BUY Before you buy a sound board, make sure your computer has room for it. Your computer must have an open expansion slot for the board to plug into. Remove the computer's cover and look inside. It should have one or more expansion slots, as shown in Figure 17.1. Some of these slots may already be occupied. In order to install a sound board, one of the slots must be free.

Also, if you are buying a sound board to play the sounds for a program you already have, make sure the sound board you purchase is compatible with the program you intend to use it with. Read the hardware requirements on the box that your program came in to determine which board you need.

WHAT'S INVOLVED? Although installing a sound card in your computer seems like a big deal, it is quite easy. You do, however, have to take the following precautions:

INFORMATION
Expansion board. An expansion board (also called an *expansion card*) is a flat piece of plastic or fiberglass that has several electronic elements soldered to it.

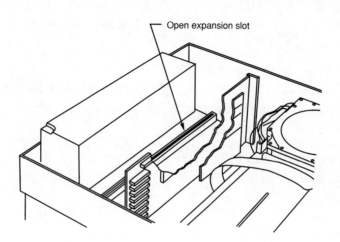

Open expansion slot

Figure 17.1 Your computer must have an open expansion slot.

- *Turn the system off.* Make sure you turn your system off and unplug everything from the power source.

- *Handle the board carefully.* A sound board (just as any expansion board) is fragile. Be careful not to break the board or break off any parts on the board.

- *Discharge static electricity.* Before you remove the board from its protective bag, touch the metal case of your computer. This discharges any static electricity to prevent it from harming the elements on the board. Handle the board only by its edges—don't touch any parts that are soldered to the board.

- *Don't touch.* Don't touch anything inside the computer. If you are charged with static electricity, touching a part inside the computer can damage it.

The procedure for installing any expansion board is basically the same for any board:

1. Remove the cover from your computer. This usually requires removing a few screws.

2. Find an open expansion slot inside the computer that is the same size as (or longer than) the board, and remove its cover. This usually requires removing a single screw.

3. Touch the metal case inside your computer to discharge static electricity, and then remove the sound board from its bag (touch only the edges of the board).

4. Plug the sound board into the expansion slot so that the receptacles on the board stick out the back of the computer (see Figure 17.2). Easy does it; don't force the board into place!

5. Secure the board in place with the screw you removed to remove the expansion slot cover.

6. Replace the cover on your computer.

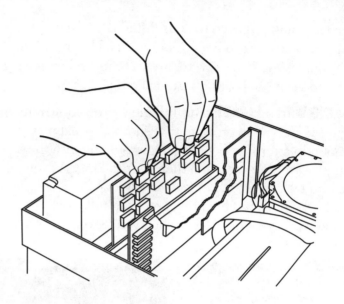

Figure 17.2 Plug the expansion board into an expansion slot.

Once the board is in place, you have to run out to the nearest electronics store and get a set of speakers or earphones, unless you already have a set lying around the house. Plug them into the back of the sound board as shown in the manual that comes with the board.

If you have a stereo system, you can use the wires that come with SoundBlaster to hook SoundBlaster into your stereo system. You can then use the volume control on the stereo. You also can get a set of speakers complete with their own volume control for about 20 bucks.

The last thing you need to do is install the various programs that come with SoundBlaster Pro. The installation procedure is the same as with any software and ends with a test to see if the board is installed properly.

TALKING WITH A PARROT The Talking Parrot, shown in Figure 17.3, is a fun program that shows the real power of SoundBlaster Pro. You plug a microphone into the SoundBlaster Pro card, and then start talking. As you talk, the bird talks back, makes its own wisecracks (such as "Yuck, you have bad breath"), and even tells you, "Goodbye, have a nice day!" when you leave.

Figure 17.3 This parrot mimics your speech.

TRANSFORMING TEXT INTO SPEECH SoundBlaster Pro comes with a program called SBTalker, a *text-to-speech synthesizer*. This takes any text you type and reads it out loud in a robotic voice. You can type single lines at the DOS prompt or you can have the program read an entire text file.

FREE ADVICE FROM DR. SBAITSO Dr. Sbaitso is an on-line psychologist with an attitude. You type in your questions or problems, and Dr. Sbaitso responds somewhat intelligently. Figure 17.4 shows what a dialog with Dr. Sbaitso looks like. The answers appear on-screen as the good doctor broadcasts them over the speakers.

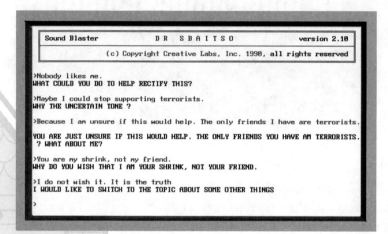

Figure 17.4 Dr. Sbaitso fields just about any question.

TAKE PIANO LESSONS FROM YOUR PC SoundBlaster Pro also comes with a program called FM Intelligent Organ, shown in Figure 17.5. The keys on your computer keyboard correspond to real piano keys; the manual illustrates just how the keys match up.

Once you start Intelligent Organ, you can press the F2 key and begin playing immediately. You then can save the song you played to disk and have the program play it back to you.

If this is your first experience with a piano or organ, you can take lessons from the program. First, load a song you want to play—"Mary Had a Little Lamb" or "Three Blind Mice," for instance. Then press F8 and then F2 to start your lesson. FM Intelligent Organ displays a screen showing you which keys to press to play the song.

Figure 17.5 An on-screen organ.

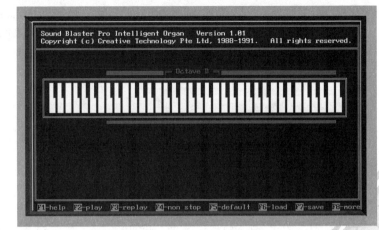

In addition, Intelligent Organ lets you switch instruments—piano, organ, flute, violin, and so on—add accompaniments, and change the tempo. With Intelligent Organ, you become the composer.

CHANGE YOUR VOICE If you have a microphone, you can use SoundBlaster's Voice Editor to record and modify your voice. You simply record your voice and then run the editor, as shown in Figure 17.6. You can then increase or decrease the volume, add an echo to the voice, change the sampling rate (to change the tone and pitch of the voice), fade the voice in or out, or pan the voice from the left speaker to the right. Advanced options let you cut and paste portions of the recording to create your own sound collages.

MULTIMEDIA—A DEMONSTRATION ON DISK Multimedia is a hot topic these days, but what exactly is it? Multimedia is a technology that allows you to join sound, pictures, animation, text, and other forms of communication in a single presentation. For example, if you get a multimedia encyclopedia on a CD-ROM disk, the encyclopedia will include text and pictures, as any encyclopedia does, but it

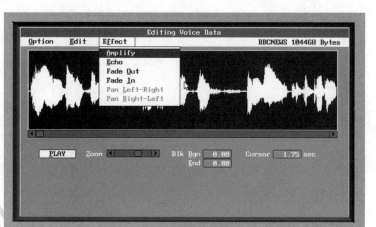

Figure 17.6 You can change your voice.

also may include music, voices, animated sequences, and even short movie clips. You'll learn more about multimedia in Chapter 19.

SoundBlaster Pro helps prepare you for the world of multimedia by including a program called MMPlay. This program lets you combine the sound features of SoundBlaster Pro with animation sequences produced using Autodesk's Animator program (which you must purchase separately). Although this stuff is beyond the casual computer user, SoundBlaster Pro includes a demonstration file that shows you what multimedia is all about.

PRACTICAL USES? NAH Okay, I admit it. Having a talking parrot on your computer screen isn't the most practical thing you can do with your computer around the house. And maybe you won't make much use of a text-to-speech synthesizer, but SoundBlaster Pro does provide a little excitement for that right side of your brain. And that in itself makes it a valuable home product.

18

CONNECTING WITH THE OUTSIDE WORLD VIA MODEM

Does your computer spend too much time alone? Is it totally oblivious to what's going on in the world? If so, consider connecting it to the phone line using a modem. With a modem and the proper software, you can use your computer to play a game with a friend in another town, look up books at the local library, check the news and weather, research a topic in an encyclopedia, buy and sell stocks, and even order items from a catalogue. In this chapter, we look at what it takes to get your computer on-line and some of the resources you can tap into.

WHAT YOU'LL NEED TO GET STARTED Before you can start placing calls, you need to gather the following items:

- *Modem.* You can get an internal or an external modem. An internal modem is a board that plugs into an expansion slot inside your computer. To use an internal modem, you must have an open expansion slot inside your computer (refer to Chapter 17). An external modem plugs into a serial port (a receptacle) on the back of your computer. To use an external modem, you must have an extra serial port; if the mouse is plugged into the serial port, you can unplug it and use that port.

- *Communications software.* Your computer needs instructions that tell it how to communicate using the modem. Most modems come with such a program, but you usually need a more sophisticated program, such as PROCOMM PLUS or the Terminal program that comes with Windows.

- An *open phone jack.* You need to plug your computer into a phone jack, just as you do with a telephone. If you don't have a phone jack near your computer, you have to install an additional jack or move your computer. It's not that hard to do; visit your local electronics equipment store to find out what it takes and refer to Figure 18.1.

INSTALLING A MODEM Modem installation varies depending on whether you are installing an internal or external modem. With an internal modem, you must get under the hood of your PC and plug the modem into an open expansion slot. From there, you have two connections to make:

1. *Modem to phone jack.* Connect the modem to the phone jack the same way you plug a phone into a phone jack.

TIP
Internal or external? Get an internal modem if you have room inside your computer and if you plan on using the modem on only one computer; otherwise, get an external modem.

INFORMATION
Just like another telephone. Your modem is just like another telephone. If you are using a modem, you won't be able to use any phone on that line, and nobody will be able to call you.

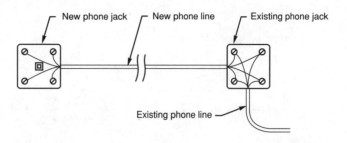

Figure 18.1 You can install another phone jack.

2. *Telephone to modem.* If you want to continue to use your telephone with this outlet, connect it to the remaining open socket on your modem.

For more information on plugging a board into an expansion slot, see Chapter 17, "Wiring Your Computer for Sound." With an external modem, you have the previous two connections to make, and two more, as shown in Figure 18.2.

1. *Modem to serial port.* Connect the modem to the serial port on your computer using a *serial cable* (you may have to purchase this cable separately).

2. *Modem to power source.* Plug the modem's power cord into a receptacle on your wall or into a power strip or surge suppressor.

> **TIP**
> **Hayes-compatible?** Make sure the modem is Hayes-compatible and that it communicates at least 2400 baud. (9600 baud is great if you can afford it.)

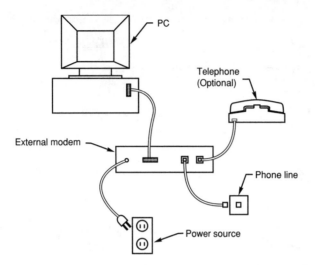

Figure 18.2 An external modem requires four connections.

BEFORE YOU CALL Before you can place a call using your modem, you need to know a little bit about the programs that make telecommunications possible. First, you must ask yourself what you want to do with the modem. The following list explains some of the common uses for a modem and the type of program required for each use:

- *Hook into on-line information services.* If you want to hook into an on-line service (such as Prodigy or America Online), you have to purchase a special program and then pay the subscription price to the service.

- *Play games in two-player mode.* If you have a game, such as Populous, that allows you to play games in two-player mode using a modem, the program already contains the tools you need to play the game over the phone lines.

- *Transfer files between two computers or connect to a bulletin board system.* You need a communications program; most modems come with a simple one. If you have PC Tools, or Windows, or some other integrated program, it may come with a communications program.

- *Compute by remote control.* If you have a computer at work and one at home, you can purchase a special remote computing program (such as Carbon Copy) that lets you control your computer at work from your computer at home and vice versa.

151

KNOW YOUR TELECOMMUNICATIONS SETTINGS If you connect your computer to another computer or to an on-line service, you must make sure both computers are using the same *communications settings*. Otherwise, errors may result during data transfer. For example, if one modem is talking at 2400 baud and the other is listening at 300 baud, it is likely that some information will get lost. Common communications settings include the following:

- *Baud rate.* This is the speed at which the two modems transfer data. The transfer can be only as fast as the slower of the two modems allows. Most 2400 baud modems can operate at slower rates (1200, 300) if needed.

- *Parity*. This tests the integrity of the data sent and received. The common setting is None or No Parity.

- *Data bits*. This setting indicates the number of bits in each transmitted character. The common setting is Eight.

- *Stop bits*. This indicates the number of bits used to signal the end of a character. The common setting is One.

- *Duplex*. This setting tells the computer whether to send and receive data at the same time (Full), or send data or receive data but not both at the same time (Half). The common setting is Full.

The important thing to remember is that the communications settings must be the same on both computers. Once the settings are right, you can use the communications program to dial the phone number and establish the connection between the two computers.

INFORMATION AT YOUR FINGERTIPS I used to get the newspaper every day. I would check out three things: the weather, my horoscope, and any stories that happened to catch my eye. That took all of about 20 minutes, and then I would dump the paper. With Prodigy, I can now get up-to-the-minute weather reports, a list of hot news stories,

CAUTION
Keep tabs on your phone bill. If you use a modem to call long distance, your friendly neighborhood phone company charges you long distance rates, so keep this in mind when you are chatting.

sports scores, my horoscope, and more at the press of a key, as shown in Figure 18.3.

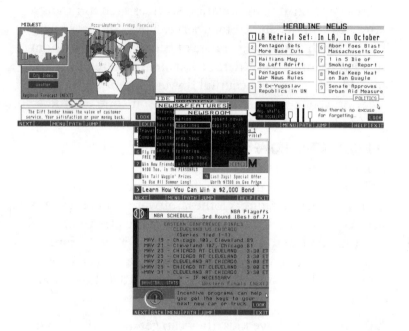

Figure 18.3 You get news, weather, and sports on-screen.

TIP
Local long distance. Most on-line information services provide you with a local number for connecting to the service. You then can communicate with other people in different states by way of the local connection.

In addition, I can look up articles in the on-line encyclopedia, check out *Consumer Reports* articles about various products, read and respond to the classifieds, get information about various health-related topics, get the latest news concerning the stock market, take any of several quizzes concerning a wide range of topics, and much more—all for about 13 bucks a month.

MEETING PEOPLE WITH SIMILAR INTERESTS Millions of people subscribe to on-line information services such as Prodigy, America Online, and CompuServe. These services put you in touch with a wide range of people, many of whom share your interests. Whether you are interested in restoring old cars, growing beautiful flower gardens, or hacking away on your computer, you can find someone out there who is doing the same thing.

THE ULTIMATE IN HOME SHOPPING Prodigy is packed with companies that are thirsty for your business and who make ordering a list of items as simple as pressing a few keys. You can order furniture, clothes, software, computer gadgets, compact discs, movies, and anything else you have a yen (or a dollar) for. As long as you have a credit card that's not maxed out, you can order anything you need, and many things you don't need. Figure 18.4 shows how easy it is.

KID STUFF If you have kids, they can get a lot out of an online service as well. Prodigy offers several illustrated children's stories that let the kids make choices along the way. For example, the story may place Goldilocks in front of a door and ask the child if Goldilocks should go through the door or turn around and run away. The child decides the outcome of the story according to his or her choices (see Figure 18.5).

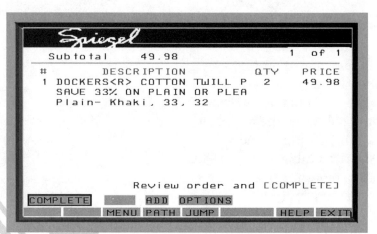

Figure 18.4 You can order a wide range of products.

Figure 18.5 The reader can play an active role.

In addition to stories, Prodigy offers science news, instructions for do-it-yourself projects, a weekly reader, history lessons, an encyclopedia, a rundown of current events, and several games just for kids. Prodigy also contains a kids club where children can converse with one another (no adults allowed). And if you are a parent, don't worry too much about your kids hearing something they shouldn't; Prodigy keeps tabs on what they say and warns them up front not to say anything they wouldn't say to their mother.

SUBSCRIPTION RATES When shopping for an on-line service, compare subscription rates. For example, Prodigy charges a flat monthly rate (about $13) that allows you to use the service as much as you want during the month and send up to 30 messages per month. Additional messages cost a quarter apiece. With America Online, you pay a flat rate (about $10) for three hours a month, $5 for each additional hour at night or on weekends, and $10 for each additional hour during weekdays.

Why does Prodigy cost less? First off, it is slower. All those fancy graphics and advertisements it displays on-screen take time to generate. Second, it displays an ad on every screen, which takes up a lot of your precious screen space and gets annoying after awhile. Compare the Prodigy screens shown throughout this chapter with the America Online screen shown in Figure 18.6.

BROWSING THROUGH THE LIBRARY The Indianapolis Public Library offers a service that allows you to connect to the library and look for books using your modem. (You don't need an on-line service, but you do need a communications program.) Although you cannot read the books, you can figure out if the library has a book, if it is out on loan, when it is due back, and which branch has it. If your local library has such a service, take advantage of it—the service can save you a lot of time in futile visits to the library.

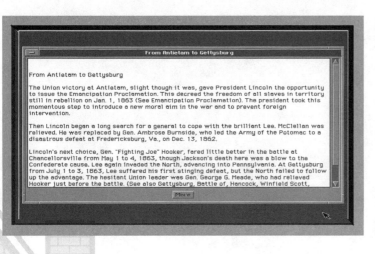

From Antietam to Gettysburg

From Antietam to Gettysburg

The Union victory at Antietam, slight though it was, gave President Lincoln the opportunity to issue the Emancipation Proclamation. This decreed the freedom of all slaves in territory still in rebellion on Jan. 1, 1863 (See Emancipation Proclamation). The president took this momentous step to introduce a new moral aim in the war and to prevent foreign intervention.

Then Lincoln began a long search for a general to cope with the brilliant Lee. McClellan was relieved. He was replaced by Gen. Ambrose Burnside, who led the Army of the Potomac to a disastrous defeat at Fredericksburg, Va., on Dec. 13, 1862.

Lincoln's next choice, Gen. "Fighting Joe" Hooker, fared little better in the battle at Chancellorsville from May 1 to 4, 1863, though Jackson's death here was a blow to the Confederate cause. Lee again invaded the North, advancing into Pennsylvania. At Gettysburg from July 1 to 3, 1863, Lee suffered his first stinging defeat, but the North failed to follow up the advantage. The hesitant Union leader was Gen. George G. Meade, who had relieved Hooker just before the battle. (See also Gettysburg, Battle of, Hancock, Winfield Scott,

More

Figure 18.6 With America Online you don't get a sales pitch on every screen.

THE LOCAL CONNECTION If you don't want to pay a subscription price to an on-line service, you may be able to connect to a local bulletin board for free or for a fraction of the cost. Don't expect to get the fancy features of costly on-line service, but the local bulletin board may let you share files with local computer users, make valuable local contacts, and get help for your computer woes. To find out about local bulletin boards, call around to various computer dealers. If they don't know of any local bulletin boards, they may know of some computer clubs you can ask. You may even want to set up your own bulletin board.

JUST TRY IT When I first got a modem, I was a little afraid to use it. The whole idea seemed much too complicated, and getting started is a little complex. To the true beginner, I suggest you find a Prodigy deal in a magazine or at a discount store. (I've seen a deal where you can get Prodigy and a modem for a reasonable price.) The book that comes with the service explains everything very clearly. Try the service for a month. Once you get comfortable with this easy-to-use service, you'll be ready to move on to more challenging arenas.

19

CD-ROM: A LIBRARY ON A DISK

How would you like to have a 26-volume set of encyclopedias on a single disk? Encyclopedias that can play snippets of Mozart's symphonies, show full-color pictures on your screen, and let you look up an article just by typing a portion of its name? How about a world atlas that provides a view of the globe along with information about each country? Or maybe you would like a book about mammals that lets you hear lions roar and monkeys chatter and lets you view the animals moving in their natural habitats? You can get all this and more for about 700 bucks with Sony's LaserLibrary.

WHAT IS CD-ROM? CD-ROM stands for Compact-Disk Read-Only Memory, and is pronounced *see-dee-ROM*. It is a storage technology that uses the same kind of disks you play in an audio CD player. The disks are made of hard plastic and measure about $4^1/_2$ inches in diameter. In addition to music, CD-ROM disks store computer files and programs. A single disk can store over 600 megabytes of information, which is equivalent to a complete set of encyclopedias.

SETTING UP—IT'S A SNAP The Sony LaserLibrary is easy to set up, assuming you have an open expansion slot in your computer. If you're not sure you have an open slot or even what an open expansion slot is, refer to Chapter 17, "Wiring Your Computer for Sound." The process of installing an expansion board in a computer is nearly the same for all expansion boards, and the LaserLibrary comes with complete instructions. Once the board is in place, you must perform a few simple steps:

1. With the power to the computer *off*, connect the CD-ROM player to the port on the expansion board.

2. Plug the CD-ROM player into a power source.

3. Connect the headphones that come with the unit.

4. Boot your computer and run the installation program that came with the unit. (The installation program comes on a floppy disk.)

The installation program will lead you through the installation process. The Demo program gives you a guided tour of the LaserLibrary, complete with sound and stylish graphics. You can use any of the following disks that come with the program to get information and play games:

- *Compton's Family Encyclopedia*
- *Microsoft Bookshelf*

INFORMATION
Read only, no writing. As the term CD-ROM implies, you can only read information from the disk into your computer. You cannot save programs or files to the CD-ROM disk.

- *Languages of the World*
- *National Geographic Mammals*
- *Mixed-Up Mother Goose*
- *World Atlas and Demo*

AN ENCYCLOPEDIA WITH SOUND Picture this. You've just seen a great movie called *Amadeus*, and you want to find out more about the protagonist in the movie: Wolfgang Amadeus Mozart. You run LaserLibrary, select Compton's Family Encyclopedia, and insert the Encyclopedia disk into the CD-ROM drive. You choose Title Finder, type **Mozart**, and press Enter. A list of titles appears, one of which is for Amadeus Mozart.

You select MOZART, Wolfgang Amadeus, and immediately an article about Mozart appears on the screen, as shown in Figure 19.1. You click on the word Picture, and a painting of Mozart appears on-screen, as shown in Figure 19.2. You click on the word Sound, and *Eine Kleine Nachtmusik* starts playing through the earphones.

A COMPLETE REFERENCE LIBRARY Disk 2 in the LaserLibrary is the Microsoft Bookshelf 1991 edition. It contains the following six reference books, which you can use for home, office, or school:

Figure 19.1 The selected article appears on-screen.

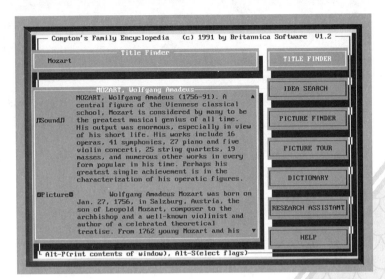

Figure 19.2 Compton's Family Encyclopedia.

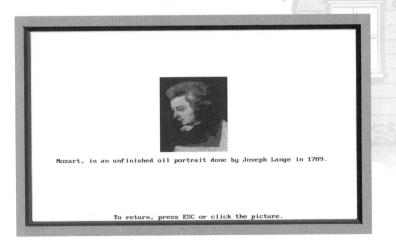

- *The American Heritage Dictionary.* This contains definitions for over 66,000 words. To find a definition, select American Heritage Dictionary from the Definitions menu, type the word you want to look up, and press Enter. No more flipping pages.

- *Roget's II Electronic Thesaurus*. Need another word for *lazy?* Simply press Alt-E, type **lazy**, and press Enter. The thesaurus gives you a list of suggestions. You then can choose a word from the list to view a list of that word's synonyms.

- *1991 World Almanac and Book of Facts*. This electronic book contains a hodgepodge of information about the world, including census figures, U.S. economics figures, employment figures, offbeat news stories, scientific achievements for 1990, and much more.

- *Barlett's Familiar Quotations*. If you like snappy quotes and insights from famous poets, politicians, and other visionaries, you'll love this book. In addition to offering the famous quotes from the paper version of the book, the CD-ROM version makes it much easier to look up quotes by author or by using a word from the quote.

- *Concise Columbia Book of Quotations*. This book offers 6,000 quotes that are appropriate for speeches and presentations. The quotes are organized by subject, so you can look up quotes for subjects such as War, City Life, and even Living Together.

- *Concise Columbia Encyclopedia*. This encyclopedia offers 15,000 pages of articles about historical

163

INFORMATION
Cutting and pasting text from the books. After looking up a definition, synonym, or quote, you then can select it, copy it to the clipboard, and paste it into the document you are working on in your word processing program.

INFORMATION
Cross-references. Many of the articles contain hypertext links that let you quickly look up related information. You simply click on the link to go to the related article.

topics, including everything from Greek mythology to the Iran-Iraq war.

A SET OF FOREIGN LANGUAGE DICTIONARIES Want to know how to say "Merry Christmas" in German? Translate words from English to French, German, Spanish, Dutch, Finnish, and other languages? Then the Languages of the World disk (Disk 3) is for you. With it, you select a source language and destination language, select a dictionary, type the word you want to translate, and press Enter.

A TRIP TO THE ZOO The fourth disk in the LaserLibrary, National Geographic's MAMMALS, is, by far, the best disk in the collection for showing what multimedia is all about. For each mammal in the series, you get to see one or more snapshots of the mammal, hear how it sounds, and/or view a movie clip of the mammal moving in its natural habitat (see Figure 19.3). The sounds of some of the mammals are eerie; the purr of the cheetah, if you can call it a purr, almost made my hair stand on end.

PLAYING GAMES WITH MOTHER GOOSE AND HER FAMILY
Disk 5 in the LaserLibrary is a game for kids called *Mixed-Up Mother Goose*. Several famous nursery rhyme characters have gotten separated from their favorite objects. Jack Be Nimble has lost his candlestick, Little Miss Muffet has lost her tuffet, and Jack and Jill have lost their pail. It's up to you to find each object and return it to its rightful owner. When you succeed, the nursery rhyme character rewards you with a little ditty, as shown in Figure 19.4.

Figure 19.3 You can see the animal move and hear how it sounds.

Figure 19.4 Mixed-Up Mother Goose is great for kids.

TRAVELING THE WORLD

Disk 6 in the LaserLibrary contains several additional items, including a demonstration program that introduces you to the LaserLibrary, several musical selections (so you can listen to music CDs while you work), and the Software Toolworks World Atlas. The Atlas, as shown in Figure 19.5, lets you get information about various

Figure 19.5 The Software Toolworks World Atlas.

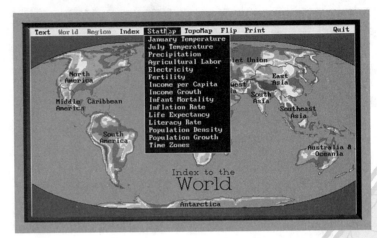

countries and cities around the globe. This information includes maps, views of the topography of a region including mountains and lakes, information about the politics of the region, statistics about population and economics, and more.

TOO EXPENSIVE? About six years ago, when my son was still floating around in embryonic fluid, my wife and I bought a set of encyclopedias for $1,500. We didn't want Junior growing up stupid. We never will get rid of these encyclopedias, because they stand as a reminder that we should never say yes to a salesperson before we talk it over together alone. At any rate, when I first saw the LaserLibrary, complete with a 26-volume encyclopedia on a disk plus five other disks for less than half what we paid for the encyclopedias, I just about had a cow.

Then, when I hooked up the CD-ROM drive to my computer and got to see what a multimedia encyclopedia could do, I *did* have the cow. So, take it from a guy who hates sales pitches—the LaserLibrary is well worth the 700 bucks.

20

ALL THIS AND AN EDUCATION TOO?!

Throughout this book, I have treated the computer as an expensive toy, as an object of awesome powers that can help you do all sorts of neat things around the house. But the computer can be used as an educational tool as well, helping children reinforce the skills they learn in school. In this chapter, we take a look at a few of the more popular educational programs on the market.

WHAT ARE EDUCATIONAL PROGRAMS? I hold a very broad definition of educational programs. To me, anything that helps a child hone a skill or inspires a child to seek more information or even just *think* is educational. In this sense, everything from math drills to arcade games is educational. The math drills may teach the child a skill as it is traditionally taught in school, but the arcade games teach hand-eye coordination, help the child tune his or her fine-motor skills, and challenge the child to develop strategies. They may even indirectly teach the child some more

TIP
Listen to your kids. Before you buy an educational program, ask your kids what they want. Kids won't learn anything from a program if they won't play it.

traditional skills. With that in mind, let's look at some of the most popular educational programs on the market.

EARLY LEARNING IN THE PLAYROOM The Playroom is a good program for preschoolers and kindergartners. When the child starts the program, he or she is placed in the play-room, shown in Figure 20.1. The child is not given any instructions, but must explore the room in order to find out what's in it. When the child clicks on an object in the playroom, the object comes to life or the child is lifted to another room where he or she can play any of the following educational games:

> **TIP**
> Play together. The Playroom is an excellent place for parent and child to play together. As a parent, you can bring out a lot more in the game by reinforcing the lessons it teaches.

Figure 20.1 With The Playroom, your child is free to explore.

- *Telling time.* Click on the clock and you get both a standard and digital clock. The child can click on the standard clock to move the hands. Pepper Mouse (a character on-screen) shows an appropriate action for the time of day selected, and a cuckoo bird comes out and chimes the hour.

- *Number recognition*. Click on the radio, and two spinners appear on-screen. One has various numbers and the other has pictures. The child learns the connection between a written number and an actual number of objects.

- *Matching*. Click on the elephant toy, and a character appears that is divided into three sections: top, bottom, and middle. The child can experiment with changing the various parts of the character until all the parts match.

- *Board game*. Click on the mouse hole, and a board game appears. Each player rolls three dice and then gets to choose one of the dice to move that number of squares. Some squares throw the player back, so it takes an ability to count and some strategy to win (see Figure 20.2).

- *Story telling*. Click on the books, and a storyboard appears with a scene from a fairy tale or a town. The child types or clicks on letters on the screen to select and place various objects and characters into the scene, creating a unique story.

- *Letter recognition*. Click on the computer, and a keyboard appears. The child can press the keys on the keyboard to see the corresponding letters appear on-screen. Click on Pepper Mouse, and a series of word boxes appear. Click on a box, and Pepper leads you through the spelling of the word.

Figure 20.2 The board game requires the child to count and form a strategy.

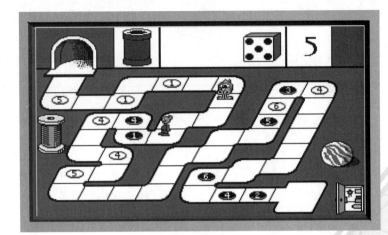

LEARNING TO READ FROM A RABBIT Reader Rabbit and Reader Rabbit 2 contain several games to help develop early reading skills, including phonics. In Reader Rabbit 2, for example, the child can play four games to help acquire and sharpen reading skills:

- *Word Mine.* The child is required to match two words to create a compound word, or to complete words using two-letter blends, such as *st* and *ck*. When the child completes a word, it falls into the mining cart.

- *Vowel Pond.* At the Vowel Pond, the child fishes for words that have specific short and long vowel sounds, as shown in Figure 20.3.

- *Match Patch.* In the Match Patch live some wily gophers. The child must look under the carrots in the patch to find matching synonyms, antonyms, or rhyming words.

- *Alphabet Dance.* In the Alphabet Dance, the child has to move characters around on the

INFORMATION
Math skills, too. The same makers of Reader Rabbit 2 market a math program called, appropriately enough, Math Rabbit.

dance floor so that their words are in alphabetical order.

Figure 20.3 Your child can learn phonics in the vowel pond.

TRAVELING THE GLOBE WITH CARMEN SANDIEGO Where in the World Is Carmen Sandiego? and the other Carmen Sandiego games (Where in the U.S.A....?, Where in Time...?, and so on) challenge children to become detectives. In Where in the World Is Carmen Sandiego?, Carmen or one of her fellow V.I.L.E. agents has committed a crime, and it's up to the player to solve the crime and find and arrest the criminal.

At the start, Interpol assigns the player a case to solve in a specific amount of time. Throughout the game, the player receives clues from various people, as shown in Figure 20.4. The player must make the connection between the clue and where on the globe that clue refers to.

Figure 20.4 Follow the clues to appre-
hend the criminal.

To help, each Carmen
game comes with a book
that contains information
about the world or about
history. In Where in the
World, for example, the
player may need to look in
the *World Almanac and
Book of Facts* to determine
a country that matches the
flag in the clue. This forces the player to go to resources
outside the game in order to win, which makes the player
learn a little about how to research various topics.

MORE INFORMATION FOR PARENTS AND TEACHERS This chapter (and this entire book, for that matter) provides a brief
introduction to the educational programs that are currently on the market. If you want to learn more about using a
computer to help your children learn, pick up *Kids &
Computers: A Parent's Handbook*, by Judy Salpeter (pub-
lished by Sams). This book contains information from
child development experts about using the computer
with your child. It answers many of the questions that
concerned parents have about computers, offers advice on
purchasing computers for your family, and provides in-
depth software reviews of a wide range of educational
programs.

TIP
Young and old alike. The
Carmen games are chal-
lenging and interesting for
all ages. We often play as a
family—one person looks
up information in the
World Almanac while the
others gather more clues.

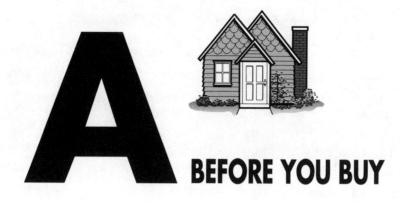

A BEFORE YOU BUY

Before you run out and buy an expensive CD-ROM player or a sound board, or even an inexpensive program, there are a few things you should know about what you are getting. For instance, you should know whether the item you are about to purchase is compatible with your system: can your system run the program? This appendix provides you with some helpful information about the hardware and software covered in this book.

NEVER PAY THE SUGGESTED RETAIL PRICE The first lesson in computer shopping is "Don't pay the suggested retail price, and avoid buying directly from the manufacturer." Software and hardware manufacturers commonly set a high suggested retail price for their products so dealers can offer great bargains. You usually can get a program for one-third to one-half off the suggested retail price by buying it through a mail-order company or through a discount software store, such as Egghead Software or Software Etc.

You also may be able to get discount commercial software at a shopping club such as Sam's Club. You can get non-commercial software, called *shareware*, from various shareware dealers or by copying programs from bulletin board services or other online services, assuming you have a modem. You can get shareware for the cost of the disk and shipping, and you are given the rights to use the shareware on a trial basis and share it with your friends. If you want to continue using the shareware, you are legally obligated to pay the developer a nominal fee, normally about $15 to $50.

READ THE BOX Before you buy a program or a piece of equipment, read the Hardware and Software requirements on the box. These requirements tell you the type of system you need in order to use the product. The box usually lists two sets of requirements: minimum and recommended. Here is a summary of some requirements for programs:

- *Computer Type (IBM, Macintosh, Apple II)*. This describes the type of computer needed to run the program. You can't run IBM programs on a Macintosh or vice versa, unless you have a special Macintosh, such as the PowerBook.

- *Memory*. Your computer has only a certain amount of memory, also referred to as *RAM (random access memory)*, in which to store active programs. To see how much memory your computer has, type mem at the DOS prompt and press

TIP
Look through a magazine. If you don't know of any mail-order companies, buy a magazine such as PC Computing and call one of the mail-order companies that have an ad in the magazine. They will be happy to send you a catalogue.

NOTE
Contrary to the way most people treat it, shareware is not freeware. With shareware, you are obligated to pay for the program eventually. With freeware (also called public domain software), you are not required to pay.

Enter. Look at the first line that appears on-screen.

Some system requirements state the total amount of memory your computer must have, whereas others state the amount of free memory. If the memory requirements specify free memory, then look at the line that says `largest exe- cutable program size` in order to determine the amount of free memory.

- *Operating System (type and version number).* To run any program, your computer must be running the right operating system, such as DOS, UNIX, or OS/2. Your operating system must also be the right version, for example DOS 3.0 or higher.

- *Microsoft Windows Required?* To run a program that requires Microsoft Windows, your system must be able to run Windows and you must have Windows installed.

- *Monitors (Monochrome, Hercules, CGA, MCGA, VGA, Super VGA).* Some programs require color monitors that can display graphics. If you have a monochrome monitor that does not display graphics, you may not be able to use the program or you may not get the most out of it.

- *Hard Disk (required or recommended).* If a program requires a hard disk, you cannot use the program without one. The program files are probably in a compressed format on the floppy disks, and you must decompress them onto the hard disk to make them usable. If a program recommends a hard disk, it's telling you that if you don't have a hard disk, you'll have to swap disks while running the program.

- *Floppy Disk Size and Capacity.* Some software for the IBM may contain only one size disk: either 3.5" or 5.25". If the disks included do not fit your computer, you have to send in a coupon requesting an exchange. Other packages get around this problem by including both sizes. In addition, if your computer has only low-density floppy disk drives, make sure you don't get a program that comes on high-density disks; you won't be able to use them.

TIP
How much disk space? To find out how much free space is on the disk, type **chkdsk** at the DOS prompt and press Enter.

The following sections list the minimum requirements for most of the products covered in this book. Unless otherwise noted, all programs are for IBM-PC or compatible computers.

America Online

512K RAM
DOS 2.0 or higher
Hercules, CGA, EGA, VGA, or MCGA graphics adapter and monitor
Hayes-compatible modem 1200 or 2400 bps

American Heritage Dictionary

43K RAM (in addition to what your other program takes)
DOS 2.1 or above
Hard disk with 3M free space

AutoMap

512K RAM
DOS 2.2 or above
Hard disk drive with 4M free space
Hercules, CGA, EGA, VGA, or Super VGA graphics adapter
and monitor

BannerMania

Hercules, CGA, EGA, ETGA, or VGA graphics adapter
and monitor
DOS 2.1 or above

Express Publisher (Windows version)

286 processor or higher
DOS 3.3 or better
Microsoft Windows 3.0 or better
2M RAM
EGA, VGA, or Super VGA graphics adapter and monitor
Hard disk with 5 to 13M free space
Microsoft or Logitech mouse

Express Publisher 2.0 (DOS version)

640K RAM
DOS 3.3 or above
Hercules, CGA, MCGA, EGA, TGA, or VGA graphics adapter
and monitor
Hard disk with 2 to 4M free space
Microsoft or Logitech mouse

Family Tree Maker 2.0

DOS 2.0 or higher
512K RAM
Mouse (optional)

The Far Side Calendar for Windows

Microsoft Windows 3.0
Hard disk with 2M free space

GeoWorks

512K RAM
Hard disk with 7 to 9M free space
CGA, MCGA, EGA, VGA, Super VGA, or Hercules Graphics
Adapter and monitor
Printer that is supported by GeoWorks
PC or MS-DOS 2.0 or above
Mouse

Health and Diet Pro

640K RAM
DOS 2.1 or over
Hard disk

Home Medical Advisor

512K RAM
DOS 3.0 or above
EGA or VGA graphics adapter and monitor
Hard disk

Info Select 2.0

DOS 2.0 or above
256K RAM

Micro Cookbook

384K RAM
Hard disk (recommended)

The New Print Shop

Hercules, CGA, Tandy, EGA, MCGA, or VGA graphics adapter
and monitor
DOS 2.11 or above
Color printing requires color printer and hard disk

OnTime for Windows

Microsoft Windows 3.0
Hard disk with 1M free space

OnTime 2.0 (DOS version)

320K RAM
DOS 2.1 (stand-alone mode)
DOS 3.1 or higher (memory-resident mode)

PFS: Resume and Job Search Pro

640K RAM
Hercules, CGA, EGA, or VGA graphics adapter and monitor
Mouse (optional)

The Playroom

Hercules, CGA, TGA, EGA, MCGA, or VGA graphics adapter
and monitor
512K RAM
DOS 2.1 or above
Supports mouse, keyboard, or joystick

Prodigy

512K RAM
DOS 2.0 or higher
Hercules, CGA, EGA, VGA, or MCGA graphics adapter and
monitor
Hayes-compatible modem 1200 or 2400 bps

Quicken 5.0

512K RAM
DOS 2.0 or above
Hard disk or two floppy disk drives, one of which is high-density

Reader Rabbit 2

CGA, TGA, EGA, MCGA, or VGA graphics adapter and monitor
512K RAM (IBM) or 640K RAM TANDY 1000
DOS 2.0 or above
Supports mouse and Ad Lib, SoundBlaster, and Roland sound
boards

RightWriter 5

1M conventional memory
Hard disk
PC or MS-DOS 3.0 or above
Compatible word processor

Sony LaserLibrary

DOS 3.1 or above
Hard disk with at least 3M free space
512K RAM
Mouse (recommended for some applications)
Open expansion slot

SoundBlaster Pro

286 or higher processor
512K RAM
DOS 3.0 or higher
EGA or VGA graphics adapter and monitor

TurboTax 9.0

Hard disk
512K RAM
DOS 2.0 or higher

WealthStarter

512K RAM
DOS 2.0 or above
Hard disk
Mouse (optional)

Where in the World Is Carmen Sandiego?

Hercules, CGA, TGA, EGA, MCGA, or VGA graphics adapter
and monitor
512K RAM
DOS 2.11 or above

WillMaker 4.0

256K RAM
DOS 2.1 or above

Windows 3.1

Intel 8086 or 8088 processor with 640K RAM (real mode)
Intel 286 processor and 1M RAM (standard mode)
Intel 386 processor and 2M RAM (enhanced mode)
MS-DOS or PC-DOS 3.1 or above
Hard disk with 6 to 8M free space
Monitor that is supported by Windows
Printer that is supported by Windows
Mouse that is supported by Windows (recommended)

WordPerfect 5.1

Hard disk or dual floppy drives (two floppy drives of the same size)
DOS 2.0 or above
404K RAM, 512K RAM (recommended)

B

GLOSSARY OF COMPUTER TERMS

Following is a list of technical and semitechnical terms that were introduced in this book along with their definitions. If you want a more comprehensive beginning computer user's dictionary, pick up my Plain English Computer Dictionary *at your local bookstore.*

antiglare screen A screen that fits over your monitor and prevents light from bouncing off the screen into your eyes.

application Also known as *program*, a set of instructions that enable your computer to perform a specific task.

backup copy An exact duplicate of a file or disk.

baud rate The speed at which information is transferred between two computers with attached modems.

boot To get your computer up and running by loading the operating system.

bulletin board system (BBS) Software that allows one computer user to call another person's computer and leave messages or exchange files.

byte A group of eight bits that usually represents a character or a digit. For example, the byte 01000001 represents the letter A.

capacity The term commonly used to represent how much data a disk can store.

CD-ROM (Compact-Disk Read-Only Memory) A storage technology that uses the same kind of disks you play in an audio CD player for mass storage of computer data.

click To move the mouse pointer over an object and press and release a mouse button (normally the left one) once without moving the mouse.

clipboard A temporary storage area for text and graphics. You can cut or copy a section of text or a picture to the clipboard, and then paste it somewhere else in the current document or into another document.

cold boot To turn on the power to your computer with the operating system in place.

command-driven A program that requires you to memorize the keystrokes you must press to execute commands.

communications software Software that allows a computer (equipped with a modem) to communicate with other computers through the telephone lines.

compress To compact files so that they take up less space.

computer In general, any machine that accepts input (from a user), processes the input, and produces output in some form.

cursor An on-screen marker that shows where keystrokes will appear. *See also* insertion point.

cut and paste An editing feature that allows you to copy or move information from one location to another.

database A type of computer program used for storing, organizing, and retrieving information.

data bit A chunk of data passed between two computers hooked up via modems. Each data bit contains a series of bits (0s and 1s) that represent a character.

data files Files that you create containing the information you typed, as opposed to *program files* that contain instructions for the computer.

density A measure of the amount of data that can be stored per square inch of storage area on a disk.

desktop publishing A program that allows you to combine text and graphics on the same page and manipulate the text and graphics on-screen.

directory A subsection of a disk marked off to keep track of files more easily.

disk drive A device that writes data to a magnetic disk and reads data from the disk.

DOS (disk operating system) An essential program that provides the necessary instructions for the computer's parts to function as a unit. Pronounced *DAWSS*.

DOS prompt An on-screen prompt that indicates DOS is ready to accept a command. It looks something like `C>` or `C:\>`.

double-click To press and release a mouse button (usually the left one) twice quickly without moving the mouse.

download To copy a file from another computer or from an on-line service or bulletin board system. *See also* upload.

drag To hold down a mouse button (usually the left one) while moving the mouse, usually used for selecting or moving an object on-screen.

error message Information that appears on-screen when a program cannot carry out a given command.

executable file A program file that can run the program. Executable files end in .BAT, .COM, or .EXE.

expansion slot A slot on your computer's main circuit board that smaller circuit boards can be plugged into, to give your computer additional capabilities.

floppy disk A wafer encased in plastic that magnetically stores data. You insert floppy disks in your computer's floppy disk drive.

font Any set of characters that have the same typeface and type size. For example, Helvetica 12 point is a font.

Helvetica is the typeface and 12 point is the size. Pronounced *FAHNT*.

format To organize the storage areas on disk so that data can be stored on it.

freeware Programs that you can use for free. Also called *public-domain software*.

function keys The 10 F keys on the left side of the keyboard or 12 F keys at the top of the keyboard.

graphical user interface (GUI, pronounced gooey) A program that provides windows, menus, and graphic icons that represent commands. Instead of having to type a command, you select an icon or an option from a menu.

graphics Anything having to do with pictures rather than text.

hard disk A nonremovable disk that acts as a giant floppy disk drive. The hard disk drive is either *internal* (inside your computer) or *external* (connected to one of the computer's ports with a cable).

Hayes-compatible A modem that uses the standard Hayes command set for communicating with other modems over the phone lines.

hot-key A key or key combination that you can press while in a program to access another program.

hypertext Key words that are linked to related subject matter (usually on a help screen).

icon A picture that represents a program, window, or file.

import To bring a file created in one program into another program.

indicator light A light on the front of the computer that lights up whenever one of the disk drives is getting information off a disk or writing information on the disk.

insertion point A blinking vertical line used in some word processors to indicate the place where any characters you type will be inserted. An insertion point is the equivalent of a *cursor*.

install program To copy the program files to a hard disk or to floppy disks so that you can use the program on your computer.

integrated program A collection of programs that run under the umbrella of a single program.

keyboard The main input device for most computers.

kilobyte A standard unit used to measure the size of a file, the storage capacity of a disk, and the amount of computer memory. A kilobyte is 1024 bytes, or 1024 characters. Pronounced *KILL-oh-bite*.

logical drive A section of a hard disk or memory that is treated as a separate disk and is assigned its own letter.

macro A record of several commands assigned to a keystroke or to a single command.

mail merge A process that allows you to combine a single letter with a list of names and addresses to create a series of letters, all addressed to different people.

megabyte A standard unit used to measure the storage capacity of a disk and the amount of computer memory. A megabyte is 1,048,576 bytes (1000 kilobytes).

memory-resident Also known as TSR or terminate-and-stay-resident, a program that remains on-call after you leave it. You can run the memory-resident program and then load another program on top of it.

menu-driven A program in which the user enters commands by selecting commands from a menu.

modem A device that enables your computer to communicate with other computers through the phone lines.

monitor The display unit for a computer. The monitor allows the computer to communicate with the user.

mouse An input device that allows you to point to and select items on-screen.

mouse pointer An arrow or rectangle that appears on-screen and moves when you roll your mouse. You use the mouse pointer to select text, draw, and enter commands.

numeric keypad A separate section of the keyboard that contains keys for typing numbers. The numeric keypad is distinct from the number keys at the top of the keyboard.

open file To read a file from a disk into your computer's memory so that the computer and you can work with it.

operating system A set of instructions that your computer reads when you start it up that allow it to function. *See also* DOS.

overstrike mode A mode in which whatever you type replaces existing text rather than moving it over.

parity bit In modem communications, the bit used to make sure that the information being transferred is not being corrupted during the transmission.

path statement A statement that tells DOS which drive to start with and which directories to follow to get to a specified file.

peripheral device Any device that's connected to the computer's central processing unit but is not a part of that unit, including printers, modems, mice, display screens, and keyboards.

physical disk The actual disk drive that you can see and touch, as opposed to the *logical disk* drive.

point To roll your mouse on the desk until the on-screen mouse pointer is positioned on the item you want to select.

port A receptacle, usually on the back of the computer, which lets you connect various input and output devices to the computer.

printer A device that transforms the electronic text contained in a file into printed material on paper.

program Also called *application* or *software*, a set of instructions that tell your computer what to do.

prompt To request input from the user by displaying a symbol or message on-screen. Many programs prompt you to type information or make a selection.

pull-down menu A list of options that drops down from a menu bar at the top of the screen.

RAM (Random Access Memory) A computer's electronic memory (in contrast to the magnetic storage of a disk). Whenever you load a program into your computer or open a file, the computer reads information from the disk and copies it into its RAM.

retrieve a file To read a file from disk into your computer's memory so that the computer and you can work with it.

run a program To load the instructions for a program into your computer's memory so that you can use the program to perform a task.

save file To save the information from your computer's memory to a named file on disk.

scanner A device that bounces light off an image on paper and takes note of the reflected light. The scanner converts the signals it picks up into a map of dots (a bit-map) that represents the shape of the scanned characters or objects.

serial port A receptacle on the back of a computer that lets you connect a serial device (usually a modem or mouse) to your computer.

shareware Programs that you can test drive for free. If you like the program and wish to continue using it, you are legally obligated to pay the developer of the program.

shell Any program that stands between the user and another program, making the other program easier to use.

sound board A circuit board that plugs into an expansion slot inside your computer and gives the computer a greater capacity for producing sounds.

spell-checker A feature included in most word-processing programs that checks your document for spelling and typographical errors.

spreadsheet A series of boxes, called *cells*, into which you enter text, numbers, and formulas.

status bar Also called *status line*, the area at the bottom of the screen in some applications that displays information about the current activity.

stop bit A bit that acts as a space between words in modem communications. It tells the computer where one byte of data stops and the next one begins.

surge protector Also known as a *surge suppressor*, a unit that stands between the computer and the electrical outlet to prevent any sudden increases in power from damaging the computer.

switch A value you can add to a command to control the manner in which the command is carried out.

system files A set of program files that your computer needs in order to operate. Normally these files are hidden. Most users never know the files are there.

text-to-speech synthesizer A technology that converts typed text into words that the computer can say. Although speech synthesis makes the computer speak, the speech sounds robotic.

thesaurus A feature included in most word-processing programs that helps you find synonyms for selected words.

tutorial A lesson on disk or in a book that teaches you how to use a program by leading you through a series of hands-on examples.

upload To copy files from your computer to another computer. *See also* download.

warm boot Also called *reboot,* the process of reloading the computer's operating system when the computer is already running. In DOS, you can reboot by holding down the Ctrl key and the Alt key and pressing the Del key.

What If analysis The process of using a spreadsheet to see what would happen if you change a value.

wild-card character A special symbol that stands in for other characters. Wild-card characters are often used in searches to find a range of items.

window A rectangular portion of the screen that displays a separate program or document. Windowing environments, such as Microsoft Windows and GeoWorks, let you run two or more programs or display two or more documents at the same time in separate windows.

Windows Also known as Microsoft Windows, a program that runs on top of your computer's disk operating system and gives the system a friendly face. *See also* graphical user interface.

word processing The act of typing and editing text using a word processing program.

write-protect To prevent data from being written to a disk or prevent a file from being changed.

WYSIWYG (What-You-See-Is-What-You-Get) A way of displaying your work on-screen so that it resembles the work as it will appear in print. Pronounced *wizzy-wig*.

INDEX

195